Chemistry
of Drugs

DAVID E. NEWTON

Facts On File
An imprint of Infobase Publishing

One Last Time . . .
for John McArdle, Lee Nolet, Richard Olson,
David Parr, David Rowand, Jeff Williams, and John D'Emilio
Thanks for the memories!

Chemistry of Drugs

Copyright © 2007 by David E. Newton

Facts On File, Inc.
An imprint of Infobase Publishing
132 West 31st Street
New York NY 10001

Library of Congress Cataloging-in-Publication Data
Newton, David E.
   Chemistry of drugs / David E. Newton.
      p. cm—(The new chemistry)
   Includes bibliographical references and index
   ISBN-10: 0-8160-5276-X
   ISBN-13: 978-0-8160-5276-9
   1. Pharmaceutical chemistry—Juvenile literature. 2. Drugs—Juvenile
literature. I. Title
RS403.N496 2007
615.'19—dc22   2006030004

Text design by James Scotto-Lavino
Illustrations by George Barille/Accurate Art, Inc.
Project editing by Dorothy Cummings

Printed in the United States of America

MP FOF 10 9 8 7 6 5 4 3 2 1

This book is printed on acid-free paper.

CONTENTS

◆ PREFACE

The subject matter covered in introductory chemistry classes at the middle and high school levels tends to be fairly traditional and relatively consistent from school to school. Topics that are typically covered in such classes include atomic theory, chemical periodicity, ionic and covalent compounds, equation writing, stoichiometry, and solutions. While these topics are essential for students planning to continue their studies in chemistry or the other sciences and teachers are correct in emphasizing their importance, they usually provide only a limited introduction to the rich and exciting character of research currently being conducted in the field of chemistry. Many students not planning to continue their studies in chemistry or the other sciences may benefit from information about areas of chemistry with immediate impact on their daily lives or of general intellectual interest. Indeed, science majors themselves may also benefit from the study of such subjects.

The New Chemistry is a set of six books intended to provide an overview of some areas of research not typically included in the beginning middle or high school curriculum in chemistry. The six books in the set—*Chemistry of Drugs, Chemistry of New Materials, Forensic Chemistry, Chemistry of the Environment, Food Chemistry,* and *Chemistry of Space*—are designed to provide a broad, general introduction to some fields of chemistry that are less commonly mentioned in standard introductory chemistry courses. They cover topics ranging from the most fundamental fields of chemistry, such as the origins of matter and of the universe, to those with important applications to everyday life, such as the composition of foods and drugs. The set title The New Chemistry has been selected to emphasize the extensive review of recent research and advances in each of the fields of chemistry covered in the set. The books in The New Chemistry set are written for middle school and high school readers. They assume some basic understanding of the principles of chemistry that are generally gained in an introductory middle or high school course in the subject. Every book contains a large amount of material that should be accessible to the interested reader with no more than an introductory understanding of chemistry and a smaller amount of material that may require a more advanced understanding of the subject.

The six books that make up the set are independent of each other. That is, readers may approach all of the books in any sequence whatsoever. To assist the reader in extending his or her understanding of each subject, each book in the set includes a glossary and a list of additional reading sources from both print and Internet sources. Short bibliographic sketches of important figures from each of the six fields are also included in the books.

INTRODUCTION

The search for chemicals that will provide relief from pain, cure disease and infection, and offer an escape from the real world has been a part of virtually every known human culture. In the earliest period of human civilization, plants, animal products, and minerals were the major source from which such chemicals were obtained. Many of those products—ranging from natural poisons obtained from frogs and certain types of plants to rocky minerals such as compounds of arsenic to mind-altering substances derived from mushrooms and cacti—are still used in at least some parts of the world as a means of capturing prey, for the treatment of disease, or for recreational purposes. Indeed, many pharmaceutical chemists believe that the natural world contains an almost endless supply of yet-to-be-discovered chemicals that will significantly augment the world's supply of *drugs*.

People's dependence on the natural world for drugs began to change, however, at the beginning of the 18th century. During this period, chemists became adept at designing and synthesizing synthetic chemicals with properties similar to or superior to those of natural medications. Compounds originally developed for other purposes, such as dyeing, were found to have therapeutic value to humans and other animals. In addition, chemists found that making relatively minor changes in the chemical structure of a substance resulted in the formation of new compounds that were often safer and/or more efficacious than the original compounds from which they were derived. The lessons learned during these early decades of modern chemistry have continued to drive much of the drug development research that continues in the 21st century.

Chemists are also drawing on newer and more revolutionary techniques for the design and development of new drugs. For example, the procedure known as *recombinant DNA* has been used to manufacture new drugs almost from the day it was imagined. The fruits of that technique in drug development have been a bonanza for the world's pharmaceutical companies and brought relief from pain and suffering for untold numbers of humans around the world.

Today, methods of drug development are drawing on chemical techniques essentially unknown only a few decades ago. For example, some researchers think that new approaches, such as *structure-activity relationship* design and *combinatorial chemistry,* are likely to be the most powerful source of new drugs in the new century. Research programs that once cost more than a billion dollars per drug candidate and lasted upwards of 10 years have now been "streamlined" by the use of these new techniques, providing the possibility of a cornucopia of new drug products for the world's medical profession.

These developments have been accompanied by a corresponding explosion in the variety of chemical products available for recreational use. As has always been the case, such products are in high demand by a relatively small proportion of the population who look for chemicals as a way of providing them with an "out-of-body" experience. Almost without exception, however, those drugs hold the potential for producing enormous risks for one's physical, mental, and emotional health.

Drug development and research today offer some of the most challenging and exciting research available to any chemist. The fruits of that research have the potential for curing diseases, such as cancer, that have proved resistant to treatment by the medical sciences since the dawn of time. Questions as to the cost of the research needed for such accomplishments and the risk of misuse of some drugs developed by it still remain to be answered. *Chemistry of Drugs* provides an introduction to the most common processes by which chemists design and develop drugs today. It describes the chemical principles on which those processes are based along with an overview of the applications and hazards associated with a variety of drugs available both legally and illegally. This description also includes a brief review of important social, economic, and political issues related to the development and use of drugs.

A Note about Drug Nomenclature

The naming of drugs is a somewhat complex and sometimes confusing process. Most drugs have at least three names: a chemical name; a generic, or common, name; and a brand, or trade, name. The chemical name of a drug is its precise, systematic name, as determined by the rules of nomenclature established by the International Union of Pure and Applied Chemistry (IUPAC). For instance, the chemical name for the anticancer drug Taxol® is 5,20-epoxy-1,2,4,7,10,13-hexahydroxytax-11-en-9-one 4,10-diacetate 2-benzoate 13-ester with (2R, 3S)-N-benzoyl-3-phenylisoserine. That tongue-twisting name obviously does not lend itself to easy communication among scientists or the general public. So, with compounds like Taxol®, and most other drugs, a second name is invented to use in place of the exact chemical name. This generic, or common, name is always much simpler, usually consisting of a single word of no more than four syllables. The generic name for Taxol®, for example, is paciltaxel. Finally, all drugs are given a commercial or trade name under which they are sold to the general public. Such names properly begin with a capital letter (as in Taxol®) and include a symbol, ®, to indicate that they are produced under a limited license by one specific drug manufacturer. By contrast, generic drugs do not carry this symbol because they can be made by any company that wishes to produce them.

In practical situations, drugs may be known by their generic name or their trade name, or by both. In most cases, there is virtually no difference between the two kinds of products except for the way they are packaged and the additives they contain. For example, the popular drug whose generic name is acetaminophen is sold under a number of trade names, including Datril®, Excedrin®, Liquiprin®, Paracetamol, Tempra®, and Tylenol®.

1
UNDERSTANDING THE WAY DRUGS WORK IN THE BODY

Where would society be today without the modern drugstore? Also known as the *pharmacy* or, in the United Kingdom and other parts of the world, the chemist's, a drugstore is our source for literally thousands of chemicals that can be used to improve our health and well-being. And each year, dozens of new chemical compounds are added to that list of lifesaving and life-improving substances. These compounds include products for the relief of pain, the treatment of allergies and stomach disorder, protection from environmental hazards, cure of infectious diseases, alleviation of body aches and sores, the remedy for poisonous bites and toxic chemicals, and a host of other beneficial results.

The term *drug* refers to a much greater array of chemicals than these health-related substances. It also includes dozens of natural and synthetic products used for recreational or nontherapeutic purposes: mind-altering chemicals that help humans escape from the "real world." Among these compounds are stimulants (*uppers*), depressants (*downers*), and *hallucinogens*.

Early Humans Discover Drugs

The use of chemicals (drugs) for both medical and recreational purposes is hardly new. In fact, drug use seems to have been a part

1

of human society since prehistory. At first, people relied entirely on natural products for the drugs they needed and used. One can imagine how such drugs might first have been discovered. Early humans probably learned quite accidentally, for example, that chewing on the bark of a willow tree (a member of the Salicaceae family) helped relieve pain. They had no idea that the bark contains a chemical compound known as salicylic acid ($[C_6H_4(OH)(COOH)]$, the primary component of the modern-day drug we call aspirin. They just used it because it worked. Similarly, they undoubtedly found by trial and error that other natural products, such as tobacco and cocaine, when smoked or chewed, produced pleasant mental states of relaxation or excitement.

Over the centuries, people developed by such methods a list of medicinal and recreational drugs that made up the earliest informal *pharmacopoeia*, a catalog of drugs, chemicals, and medicinal preparations. Chemicals that "worked" (that brought relief, cured, or altered a mental state) made that list. Those that did not (killed people or caused serious harm) usually did not.

The pharmacopoeia of chemicals used for health purposes has changed dramatically in the past three centuries. The one area in which early humans were generally not very successful in discovering new drugs was in the search for products that would cure infectious diseases, such as pneumonia, influenza, tuberculosis, smallpox, and typhoid. Until the germ theory of disease was developed in the last third of the 19th century by the French chemist Louis Pasteur (1822–95) and the German bacteriologist Robert Koch (1843–1920), no one really understood how people became ill and died from infections, and trial-and-error methods for fighting such diseases were largely unsuccessful. After the work of Pasteur and Koch, however, a theoretical basis was created for the development of disease-fighting chemicals, even if the discovery of such drugs itself turned out to be a long and drawn-out process that is still very much under way.

Interestingly enough, the pharmacopoeia of mind-altering drugs has undergone somewhat less change than that of medicinal drugs. Some of the recreational drugs most popular with our ancestors— alcohol, tobacco, cocaine, opium (in its various forms), and psilocybin (from certain mushrooms), for example—are still widely used in modern society, in either their original or slightly altered forms.

Indeed, most of the "progress" in the development of recreational drugs has been in the search for compounds that are only modest chemical variations of centuries-old drugs. The invention of entirely new mind-altering drugs (such as lysergic acid diethylamide, or LSD) has been relatively uncommon.

Types of Drugs

Any study of drug design, development, and use today must note the basic distinctions now made between the two large categories of chemical compounds: those that have some medical benefit and those used primarily for recreational and/or nontherapeutic purposes. Of course, some compounds can fit into both categories, to one degree or another. Morphine, for example, is a valuable and important medical tool for the control of pain and, therefore, a "good" drug in some respects. It can also be used (in its natural state or an altered form known as heroin) as a dangerous, recreational, and therefore "bad" drug.

In the United States today, the legal standard by which "good" and "bad" drugs are now measured is the Controlled Substances Act of 1970. This act divides all known drugs into one of five classes, known as *schedules*. The primary criterion by which a compound is placed into one or another schedule is its potential for abuse, that is, its potential for addictive or otherwise harmful nonmedical applications. The Controlled Substances Act provides detailed descriptions of, restrictions on, and penalties for the use of chemical compounds in each of the five schedules. These schedules are defined as follows:

➤ Schedule I: Any drug with a high potential for abuse, that has no currently accepted medical use in treatment in the United States, and that lacks any accepted safety for use under medical supervision.

➤ Schedule II: Any drug with a high potential for abuse, that has a currently accepted medical use in treatment in the United States, with a potential for abuse that may lead to severe psychological or physical dependence.

➤ Schedule III: Any drug with a potential for abuse less than the drugs or other substances in schedules I and II, that has a currently accepted medical use in treatment in the United States, and for which abuse of the drug may lead to moderate or low physical dependence or high psychological dependence.

➤ Schedule IV: Any drug with a low potential for abuse relative to the drugs or other substances in Schedule III, that has a currently accepted medical use in treatment in the United States, and for which abuse of the drug may lead to limited physical dependence or psychological dependence relative to the drugs in schedule III.

➤ Schedule V: Any drug that has a low potential for abuse relative to the drugs in schedule IV, that has a currently accepted medical use in treatment in the United States, and for which abuse of the drug may lead to limited physical dependence or psychological dependence relative to the drugs in schedule IV.

Some of the restrictions on and penalties for the illegal use of compounds in each of the five schedules are shown in the chart opposite.

Drug deals are often conducted close to schools and even on school grounds. (Will and Deni McIntyre/Photo Researchers, Inc.)

◀ SOME PROVISIONS OF THE CONTROLLED SUBSTANCES ACT OF 1970 ▶

SCHEDULE	REGISTRATION REQUIRED?	PRODUCTION QUOTAS?	DISTRIBUTION REQUIREMENTS?	DISPENSING	LIMITS AND PENALTIES
I	Yes	Yes	Order forms	Research use only	0–20 years/ $1 million
II	Yes	Yes	Order forms	Written prescription; no refills	0–20 years/ $1 million
III	Yes	Generally, no; some limitations	Written records required	Written or oral prescription; limited refills	0–5 years/ $250,000
IV	Yes	Generally, no; some limitations	Written records required	Written or oral prescription; limited refills	0–3years/ $250,000

(continues)

◄ SOME PROVISIONS OF THE CONTROLLED SUBSTANCES ACT OF 1970 *(continued)* ►

SCHEDULE	REGISTRATION REQUIRED?	PRODUCTION QUOTAS?	DISTRIBUTION REQUIREMENTS?	DISPENSING	LIMITS AND PENALTIES
V	Yes	Generally, no; some limitations	Written records required	Over-the-counter drugs; prescription drugs limited to doctor's orders	0–1 year/ $100,000

Source: The Controlled Substances Act of 1970, Public Law 91–513. Provisions of the act can be accessed online at http://www4.law.cornell.edu/uscode/21/ch13.html.

In principle, the Controlled Substances Act provides a clear system for distinguishing between drugs intended for beneficial purposes and those with few or no beneficial purposes. In practice, that distinction is not always so clear. New drugs developed to treat some medical condition may also have properties that make them attractive as recreational drugs. Thus, some "good" drugs end up being used for "bad" purposes. One of the challenges to the drug industry and the law enforcement community today is finding ways of preventing drugs with useful medical purposes from being adopted by recreational drug users for illegal purposes.

How Drugs Work: Disease Prevention

The design and synthesis of new drugs today is greatly facilitated by scientists' improved understanding as to how such compounds work in the body. Researchers have long known that most drugs that cure disease do so by killing the microorganisms that cause such diseases. They now have, in many cases, a very detailed and specific understanding as to how that process occurs. Research on HIV infection and AIDS (acquired immunodeficiency syndrome) is a good example. In 1983, two researchers, Luc Montagnier in France and Robert Gallo in the United States, reported that AIDS is caused by a particular type of virus that was later given the name human immunodeficiency virus (HIV). Over the next decade, teams of researchers in many countries discovered the mechanism by which HIV causes the symptoms of AIDS.

The first step in that process occurs when a person is exposed to HIV (usually through sexual contact or transfer of blood from an infected to a healthy person). HIV travels through the bloodstream until it comes into contact with certain types of white blood cells that contain proteins known as CD4 (cluster designation 4) receptor sites on their surface. The virus then attaches itself to the CD4 receptor and injects a protein (called the p24 protein) into the host cell's interior. The p24 protein carries the genetic information that controls reproduction of HIV.

Once installed inside the host cell, the p24 protein attaches itself to and takes over control of the cell's own DNA. The HIV genetic code begins to function within the host cell, ordering it to produce multiple copies of itself (the virus). The host cell then becomes filled with new copies of the HIV, bursts open, releases the viruses into the bloodstream, and dies. Each of the new viruses thus produced then finds another CD4 host cell, and the whole process of reproduction is repeated.

Before scientists understood this process, about the only way they had of treating the symptoms of AIDS was a trial-and-error search for chemicals that appeared to have success in curing or slowing down the disease. Once the mechanism of infection was understood, however, they had a more rational method of looking for drugs with which to treat the disease. Their challenge was to find one or more chemicals that would interrupt the series of steps by which the virus operates (attaching itself to the surface of the cell, injecting its p24 protein into the cell, and initiating replication within the host cell). In fact, various researchers looked for a variety of chemical compounds that acted at one or another of these stages of infection.

The best solution that researchers have so far discovered involves the use of a type of drug known as an antiretroviral agent, that is, a chemical that interferes with the process by which the p24 protein takes over the host cell's own system of replication and reproduction. Many people who are infected with HIV are now able to live reasonably normal lives because they have access to an "AIDS cocktail" that contains some combination of three such antiretroviral substances.

Another example of how drugs kill disease-causing microorganisms is the action of sulfa drugs on bacteria, shown in the diagram on page 9. Normally, a bacterium requires a compound known as para-aminobenzoic acid (PABA) in order to make a second compound, folic acid, as shown in the diagram below. Folic acid, in turn, is used to catalyze the production of nucleic acids that become part of a bacterium's mechanism for manufacturing new proteins and reproducing its own DNA.

The structure of sulfa drug molecules, however, is very similar to that of the PABA molecule. Compare the structure of sulfanilamide, in part 2 of the diagram, with that of PABA. Notice how easily the sulfanilamide molecule can substitute for the PABA molecule in the synthesis of the bacterium's folic acid. The problem for the bacterium, however, is that folic acid produced from a sulfa drug molecule is

Mechanism of sulfa drug action: (1) Normal sequence, (2) Action of sulfa drug

different from one produced from a PABA molecule. The difference is great enough that the altered form of folic acid is unable to catalyze the synthesis of DNA, and the bacterium's metabolic process is disrupted. Unable to grow and reproduce, members of the bacterial colony die and the infection that they cause is successfully treated.

Understanding the mechanisms by which normal body functions occur, how disease develops, and how drugs fight disease is now fundamental to the development of new drugs. This understanding allows researchers to develop new chemical compounds that interfere with biochemical changes that result in disease and death.

How Drugs Work: Altering Mental Processes

A great many physical and mental disorders develop because of a malfunction in the nervous system. Some examples are Alzheimer's disease, schizophrenia, Parkinson's disease, Huntington's chorea, and bipolar disorder. Most of the effects produced by recreational drugs, such as alcohol, heroin, and cocaine, are also a result of changes in the way the nervous system functions. Today, scientists have a reasonably good understanding of the way in which the nervous system operates and how many types of chemicals affect this operation.

In simple terms, messages travel along neurons (nerve cells) in the form of an electrical current that moves from one end of the neuron to its opposite end. The electric current is produced by a flow of sodium ions (Na^+) and potassium ions (K^+) across the nerve membrane, as shown in the diagram on page 11. When the electrical current reaches the end of the neuron, it causes the release of a chemical known as a *neurotransmitter.* Some examples of neurotransmitters are acetylcholine, serotonin, dopamine, GABA (gamma-aminobutyric acid), and norepinephrine.

Neurotransmitters released at the end of one neuron travel the short distance between that neuron and another nearby neuron across a space known as the *synaptic gap,* shown in the diagram below. When the neurotransmitter reaches the second neuron, it bonds chemically to that structure, releasing a flow of electrical charges, which then travels down the second neuron.

The key to nerve transmission—like most of the biochemical reactions that occur in living organisms—is the concept of a *receptor molecule,* a molecule to which some other molecule binds. In the example just described, a receptor molecule is a specific chemical compound with a distinctive shape into which the neurotransmitter molecule can fit. The diagram on page 12 shows how a specific neurotransmitter has the correct shape to fit into a receptor molecule.

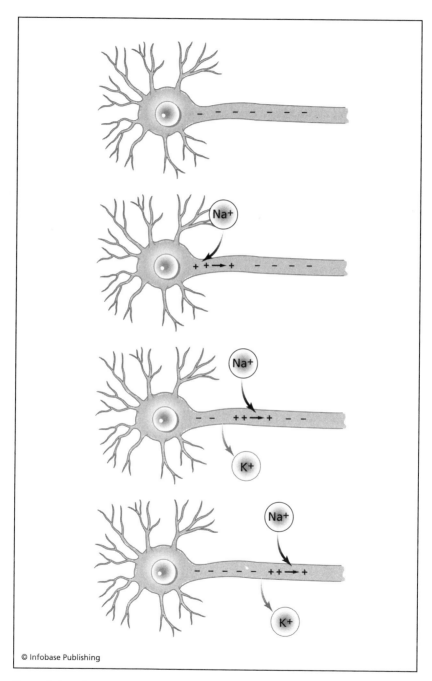

Transmission of a nerve message along a neuron

However, a similar molecule with a different shape would be unable to "dock" at the neurotransmitter molecule.

Scientists now know that many natural biological phenomena can be explained in terms of this model. The toxic or other harmful effects of certain naturally occurring substances is one example. For example, curare is an aqueous extract of the sap of a vine, *Strychnos toxifera,* used by South American Indians to poison arrow tips. The substance is also used medically as a muscle relaxant. Scientists have learned that the physiological effects of curare occur because the mixture contains at least 40 alkaloids (organic bases containing nitrogen) whose structures mimic those of certain neurotransmitters. When these alkaloids are introduced into the bloodstream, they tend to migrate to receptor cells on neurons where they bond firmly to those cells and prevent neurotransmitters from attaching themselves. When that happens, the transmission of nerve messages from one neuron to another

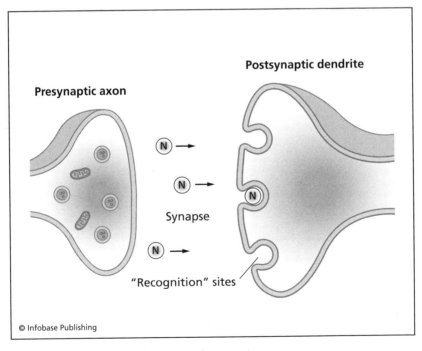

Movement of a neurotransmitter across the synaptic gap

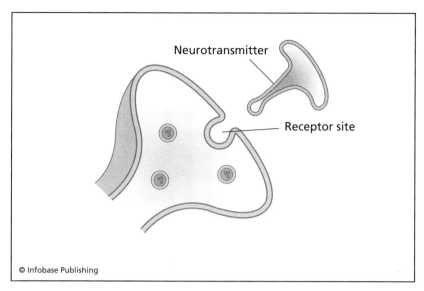

© Infobase Publishing

Docking of a neurotransmitter molecule with a receptor site

is interrupted, and the nervous system slows down or ceases to function altogether.

Some mental disorders also appear to result from disruption of the natural flow of neurotransmitters between neurons. For example, scientists now believe that the disorder known as Parkinson's disease may result from a deficiency of the neurotransmitter dopamine. Parkinson's disease is characterized by muscular rigidity, tremor while the person is at rest, difficulty in initiating movement (a condition known as *bradykinesia*), slowness of voluntary movement, difficulty with balance, and difficulty with walking. When the neuronal cells that produce dopamine begin to deteriorate, they release less of the neurotransmitter; the normal flow of dopamine between cells is reduced; and disruptions of normal nerve patterns develop, as evidenced by the symptoms described.

Assuming that this explanation of Parkinson's disease is correct, a possible treatment for the condition is apparent: Provide patients with an increased supply of dopamine. With additional levels of dopamine in the body, normal nerve function might be expected to be restored, and the symptoms of Parkinson's might be reduced. This form of therapy appears to make theoretical sense, and it has formed the basis of considerable experimental work on drugs for the treatment of Parkinson's. In practice the disorder is not so easily treated for a variety of reasons, one of which is that dopamine, in the form in which it occurs in the human body, does not pass through the blood-brain barrier that protects the brain from potentially harmful substances. So researchers are obliged to find an alternative method by which the compound can be administered to patients.

Many recreational drugs appear to exert their characteristic effects by similar mechanisms. For example, the amphetamines, cocaine, and nicotine all appear to increase the supply of dopamine in the brain, stimulating increased nerve action. Such changes account for the increase in physical activity associated with the use of these drugs. In other cases, a drug may decrease physical activity. Drugs of the class known as opiates (opium, morphine, and heroin), for example, all contain molecules whose shape allows them to bond at receptor molecules, preventing neurotransmitters from occupying those positions and consequently reducing nerve transmission in the central nervous system. This reduction in nerve action accounts for the characteristic slowing of physical responses associated with use of opiates.

One of the most promising fields of drug research is the search for chemical compounds that can relieve pain. Although the biomolecular process by which pain is produced is not fully understood, scientists now have some important clues. One currently popular hypothesis ties the transmission of pain to a chemical compound known as *substance P.* Evidence suggests that substance P is a neurotransmitter that carries a "pain message" from one neuron to an adjacent neuron. It may be responsible for the transmission of such messages from neurons in the peripheral nervous system to the brain.

A clue to possible treatments for pain was discovered in the 1970s when scientists found specialized receptor cells in neurons called *opiate receptors.* These receptors appeared to be well suited for accepting natural painkillers that occur in the body, such as the enkephalins and endorphins. Enkephalins and endorphins are naturally occurring painkillers similar in their action to opium, morphine, and codeine.

◄ OTTO LOEWI (1873–1961) ►

A German-American physiologist, Otto Loewi discovered the first neurotransmitter, acetylcholine. Loewi was born in Frankfurt- am-Main on June 3, 1873. He attended the University of Strasbourg, from which he received his medical degree in 1896. He then worked for a period of time at University College in London, the University of Vienna, and the University of Graz (Austria).

By the beginning of the 20th century, scientists had achieved a reasonably good understanding of the way messages were transmitted along neurons. They understood to a considerable degree the electrical nature of these neural communications. One remaining problem of significant proportions, however, was how such messages passed from one neuron to the next. As early as 1903, the English neurologist Thomas R. Elliott (1877–1961) proposed an answer to this problem. He suggested that chemical molecules picked up the message at the axon (end) of one neuron and carried it across the space between two neurons to the beginning (dendrite) of another. We now call such molecules *neurotransmitters,* although that name was not used until 1961.

More than two decades passed before Loewi confirmed Elliott's hypothesis. The experiment through which Loewi made this discovery in 1921 has become a classic. The story is told that during a dream in the middle of the night, he first imagined an experiment that would allow him to detect a neurotransmitter. He woke up and wrote down his plan, but in the morning he could not read what he had written. The next night, instead of going to bed, he went directly to his laboratory, where he worked out the details of his experiment and carried it through to his conclusion. By dawn of the next day, he had obtained the proof he needed for the existence of a neurotransmitter.

For his discovery of acetylcholine, Loewi was awarded a share of the 1936 Nobel Prize in physiology or medicine. As one condition of being allowed to leave Austria in 1938, he was required to hand over the cash award that was given him as part of his Nobel Prize.

When Germany invaded and conquered Austria in 1938, Loewi was placed under arrest. Fortunately, he was eventually released from prison and was able to escape the country, traveling first to Belgium and England and then to the United States. He was then appointed to a position at the New York University College of Medicine, where he remained until 1946. He died in New York City on December 25, 1961.

The diagram below shows the hypothesized mechanism by which natural painkillers bring about their effect. A pain message is transmitted from the one end (the axon) of one neuron to the end of a second neuron (the dendrite), where molecules of substance P cross the synaptic gap between the two neurons. Present in the spinal cord, however, are additional neurons capable of releasing natural opiates into the environment surrounding the sensory neurons. The presence of natural opiate molecules appears to inhibit the production and release of substance P molecules, interrupting their flow across the synaptic gap and reducing or eliminating the pain message.

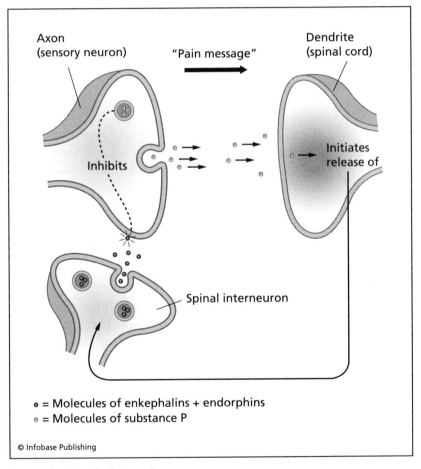

Proposed action of substance P

The development of this hypothesis, should it turn out to be correct, provides a useful blueprint for the design and development of new pain-relieving drugs. Such drugs should probably have chemical structures similar to those of naturally occurring opiates. When taken into the body, they should be able to supplement or replace the action of naturally occurring opiates in the reduction of pain.

As with research on drugs for the treatment of disease, an understanding of the mechanism by which mind-altering drugs operate is fundamental to the development of new chemicals to treat mental disorders, such as Parkinson's disease, schizophrenia, and depression. Scientists now understand that many abnormal mental conditions are the result of biochemical imbalances—an excess or deficiency of essential chemicals in the central nervous system—that can be ameliorated or cured by treatment with natural or synthetic drugs.

The Future of Drug Design and Development

The preceding discussion might seem to suggest that the design and synthesis of new drugs may now be a fairly simple and straightforward task. Researchers might focus on the search for compounds with certain specific requirements established by the shape and chemical characteristics of a given receptor molecule or of molecules involved in relevant biological processes. It might seem, for example, that a cure for AIDS would involve nothing more complex (in principle) than the design of drugs that interrupt the action of the HIV at any one of a number of critical stages of infection of a host cell.

Unfortunately this is not the case. In the first place, the mechanisms of disease, pain, altered mental states, and drug action are often very complex and still not well understood. The molecular biology and biochemistry of many systems still have not been studied or their actions unraveled. In such cases, some type of trial-and-error search for drugs still may be the only possible approach for new drug synthesis. In other cases, the number of chemical compounds that might meet the criteria for success might be so large that some method must be found for searching through and assessing all possible candidates.

◄ CANDACE BEEBE PERT (1946–   ) ▷

Over the past century, chemists have discovered the ability to explain a whole range of biological phenomena, from the mechanisms by which genetic information is passed from parents to children to the processes by which certain compounds kill microorganisms. Is there any aspect about "being human" that chemists cannot explain? Is it possible that even questions of how the brain and mind function can be answered by a better understanding of the biochemistry of the human body?

Many researchers are now attempting to answer that question. An important breakthrough in the field came in 1973 when two researchers at the Johns Hopkins University, Solomon Snyder and Candace Pert, discovered an essential key to the way in which natural body chemicals relieve pain and provide dramatic changes in the brain.

Candace Beebe Pert was born in New York City on June 26, 1946. After graduating from MacArthur High School in Levittown, New York, she enrolled at Hofstra University. She left school in 1966, however, to marry Agu Pert and to have the first of the couple's three children. Instead of continuing with her college studies, Pert took a job to help her husband complete his doctoral degree at Bryn Mawr College in Philadelphia. For some time, it appeared that Candace's own dreams of earning a college degree were not to be realized. Then in 1967, while working as a cocktail waitress, she met an administrator at Bryn Mawr, who convinced her to return to college. Three years later, she was awarded her bachelor's degree in biology and was accepted in the doctoral program in pharmacology at Johns Hopkins. She was awarded a Ph.D. in that field in 1974.

In still other cases, one might wish to design and test compounds that are chemically and biologically similar to existing drugs (either medical or recreational) but that have effects slightly different from the existing product. This is a very popular field of research, as reflected in the findings of a recent survey that showed that only about 15 percent of all the drugs approved for use in the United States by the Food and Drug Administration in the past decade are truly unique. The remaining 85 percent of these products were largely variations of existing products.

For her doctoral research, Pert investigated the mechanism by which morphine and opium exert their effects in human cells. She discovered the existence of certain receptor molecules on neurons that seemed designed for opiate-like compounds naturally present in the brain. When these natural opiates (later called endorphins and enkephalins) bond to receptor sites, they disrupt the natural flow of neural messages producing a variety of mental states, including euphoria (a "high"). Pert's later research has been directed at the mechanisms by which Valium and certain recreational drugs, such as PCP (angel dust) interact with normal neural messages in the brain.

After graduation, Pert remained at Johns Hopkins as a National Institutes of Health fellow (1974–75), staff fellow (1975–77), senior staff fellow (1977–78), and then research pharmacologist (1978–82). In 1982, she was appointed chief of the section on brain chemistry at the National Institutes of Mental Health, a post she held until 1987. In that year, she organized her own company, Peptide Design, for research on and development of peptides similar to those she had been studying for the preceding decade. In the mid-1980s, while researching the function of classical immune cell receptors in the brain, Pert and Dr. Michael Ruff, her collaborator, developed the first of a new class of treatments for HIV/AIDS, the viral entry inhibitor Peptide T. In 1990, Pert was appointed Research Professor in the Department of Physiology and Biophysics at Georgetown University Medical Center in Washington, D.C., a post she still holds. In 1999, she wrote a popular book about her research, *Molecules of Emotion: The Science Behind Mind-Body Medicine.*

Drug researchers in the 21st century still face a daunting array of tasks. The nature of these tasks and some of the progress that has been made in meeting those challenges are the topics of the remaining chapters of this book.

2

NATURAL PRODUCTS

*If blood flows from the womb, let the woman drink dark wine in which
the leaves of the vitex [chaste berry plant] have been steeped.*
—Hippocrates, ca. 440 B.C.E.

*To cure cataracts, draw fresh water from a well, add a gold or silver
coin and blades of grass. Let the mixture steep. Then pass the blades of
grass across the eye and pour water from the mixture into the eyes.*
—medieval folk remedy

*To cure an abscessed tooth, apply a piece of onion on the sore area to
draw out the infection and improve circulation to the tooth.*
—modern folk remedy

These three prescriptions cover a span of nearly 2,500 years, but
they have something fundamental in common: They call for the
use of natural products to cure illness. There have been relatively few
times and few cultures in which natural products did not play a major
role in the healing arts. Even today, in the highly modern world of the
21st century, extracts from plants and other organisms continue to be
widely used in both developed and in developing nations.

According to a study conducted by the World Health Organization
in 1988, about 80 percent of the world's population still rely almost
entirely on traditional medical techniques in which natural products
play the predominant role. The vast majority are people who live in

developing nations where the materials and procedures of modern medicine are still largely unavailable. Even in developed nations, however, natural products constitute a significant part of the available pharmacopoeia. In the United States, about a quarter of the prescription drug market, with an estimated value of $15.5 billion, is based on drugs derived from plants. Between 1983 and 1994, just over 40 percent of all new drugs approved for use in the world were derived from natural products. In the case of anti-infectives (compounds used to treat infections), the proportion was more than 60 percent.

Traditionally, plants have accounted for by far the most important source from which drugs have been obtained. A few traditional drugs have been produced from inorganic substances, such as arsenic and antimony. Beginning in the 19th century, microorganisms became another important source of drugs, but when researchers begin looking for new drugs that can be obtained from natural products, most still turn to plants.

The Use of Natural Products as Drugs in History

Natural products appear to have been used to cure illnesses almost since the beginning of time. Possibly the oldest known recipes for such cures are found on a set of 660 clay tablets from the Mesopotamian civilization dating to the third millennium B.C.E. These tablets contain a list of more than a thousand plants used for medicinal purposes.

Natural medicines were being used in China at about the same time. A famous text dating to about 1000 B.C.E., the *Huang Ti Nei Ching Su Wen* (Yellow Emperor's canon of internal medicine), is regarded as the oldest record of traditional Chinese medical techniques and describes treatments that were used as far back as about 2500 B.C.E. The oldest Chinese book containing recipes for herbal treatments is *Shen Nung Pen Ts'ao Ching* (Shen Nung's catalog of herbs), dating to about 1000 B.C.E.

Relatively little progress was made in the West in the treatment of disease from the rise of Christianity to the end of the Middle Ages, to some extent because illness was regarded as punishment for one's sins. As a result, prayer and the hope for miracles were frequently the only methods available for the cure of disease. During the Renaissance, however, a renewed interest in the use of plant materials (usually herbs) sprang up in Europe. The first pharmacopoeia in the modern era, written by the German botanist Valerius Cordus (1515–44), was published posthumously in 1546. (A pharmacopoeia is a list of drugs and medicines, with a description of the illnesses for which they are useful and instructions for their preparation.) Cordus's *Dispensatorium* was soon followed by other pharmacopoeia in other parts of Germany and other countries of Europe. The first such book in the United States, the *Lititz Pharmacopoeia,* was published by Dr. William Brown in 1778 for use in military hospitals during the American Revolution.

As in the modern world, plant materials were used not only to treat disease but also for other purposes, the most important of which was to produce hallucinogenic, psychedelic, or other "out-of-body" experiences. Many cultures throughout history have made the use of such materials an integral part of their religious ceremonies. For

One of the most widely used of all illegal drugs is marijuana, which comes from the *cannabis sativa* plant. (Ted Kinsman/Photo Researchers, Inc.)

example, ancient Hindu documents assert that the hallucinogenic effects of marijuana were first discovered by the god Shiva, who ate leaves of the plant and found them very refreshing. Thereafter, the plant was routinely used in many Hindu ceremonies, usually in a form known as *bhang.* In the New World, the peyote cactus has been used in religious ceremonies for at least 10,000 years. The cactus contains at least 40 chemicals with mind-altering properties, the most important of which is mescaline.

Plant materials have also been used as drugs in some cultures for the killing of prey or in weapons used in battle. Perhaps the best known example of such use is the practice among some South American tribes of using curare, an extract of the plant *Chondrodendron tomentosum,* as a poison for the tips of their arrows used both in hunting and in warfare. The active ingredient in curare is the chemical known as D-tubocurarine.

Other South American tribes use a poison obtained from a group of amphibians known as *poison dart frogs.* These frogs are members of the family *Dendrobatidae* and belong primarily to the genera *Dendrobates, Phyllobates,* and *Epipedobates.* The most toxic member of the group is a frog known as *Phyllobates terribilis,* whose secretions are so toxic that they can cause serious illness to a human simply through contact with the skin. The most important active ingredient in the poison excreted by poison dart frogs is a chemical known as pumiliotoxin.

Natural Products and the Rise of Modern Chemistry

Prior to the 19th century, practitioners of the healing arts knew essentially nothing about either the chemical composition of natural products or the mechanisms by which they work. They relied entirely on tradition, and trial and error, in the choices they made of the substances they used in their work.

That situation began to change in the early 1800s with the rise of organic chemistry. Researchers began to find ways to separate traditional drugs and medicines into their component parts, determine the chemicals of which they were made, elucidate their chemical structures, and, to some extent, synthesize the compounds in the laboratories.

It was a daunting task. In the vast majority of cases, the natural products traditionally used by healers are complex mixtures of dozens of chemical compounds, some of which may have medicinal properties, and some of which may not. At first, the most that chemists could hope to accomplish was to obtain one or more active ingredients of plant materials in a pure form. To determine the chemical structures of these ingredients was, at the time, far beyond their capacity. Indeed, the molecular structures of chemicals obtained in a pure form in the early 1800s were often not determined until more than a hundred years later.

For example, one of the first chemicals to be purified from a natural product for use as a drug was morphine. In 1805, the German chemist Friedrich Wilhelm Sertürner (1783–1841) isolated the compound from opium while trying to find out how that substance induces sleep. He obtained morphine in a pure form, as white crystals, but had no idea as to its chemical composition. That limitation did not prevent morphine's being put to use as a drug, however. In 1826, Emanuel Merck (1794–1855), founder of the great Merck Chemical company, began producing pure morphine commercially for use as a drug. Still, the compound's chemical structure remained a mystery for more than a century. Finally, in 1925, the English chemist Sir Robert Robinson determined the structural formula for morphine (with the exception of one uncertain atom).

Another historically significant example is the story of quinine. For centuries, quinine was the most effective drug for the treatment of malaria, which has long been one of the world's most serious and widespread infectious diseases. The substance was first used as an antimalarial treatment in the 1600s, although how it was discovered it still not known with certainty. In any case, its importance as a drug inspired the search for methods of extracting it from its natural source and determining its chemical structure so that it could be made synthetically.

The first problem was solved in 1820 when the French chemist Pierre-Joseph Pelletier (1788–1842) and his associate Joseph-Bienaimé Caventou found a way to extract quinine from cinchona bark. That accomplishment gave no clue, however, as to the compound's chemical structure, so chemists were unable to synthesize quinine *analogs* in the laboratory. (In pharmacology, an analog is a drug whose chemical structure is similar to that of another drug, but whose chemical and biological properties may be quite different.) Indeed, it was not until the 1920s that progress was made in that direction. Then researchers discovered that a number of compounds belonging to the aminoquinoline family were effective in the treatment of malaria. Between the 1920s and the 1950s, these two compounds were the most effective antimalarials available.

Still, the search for the chemical structure of quinine itself went on, a pursuit that was not successful until 1944. In that year, the American research team of Robert Burns Woodward (1917–79) and William von Eggers (1917–   ) completed the monumental task of elucidating the structure of quinine. With this knowledge, it became possible for chemists to begin producing quinine synthetically in the laboratory and, more important, to develop analogs that were even more effective than the natural product. The most effective of the quinine analogs was mefloquine, developed during the Vietnam War as the result of a program developed by the Walter Reed Army Institute for Research to protect American soldiers against malaria.

The morphine and quinine stories have established a model for the study of natural products that has been repeated many times in recent history, that is, the search for the chemical structure of a biologically active substance so that (1) the compound can then be made synthetically and (2) analogs of the drug can be produced and tested for biological activity. (The term *biological activity* refers to the beneficial or adverse effects of a drug on living materials.) One of the most exciting achievements in this type of research involved the study of a natural product that has been used by Chinese herbalists for thousands of years to treat fever. Called qing hoa, it is also known as sweet wormwood, annual wormwood, and sweet annie. Its systematic name is *Artemisia annua.* In addition to its use as an antipyretic (antifever medication), qing hoa has been used effectively as an antimalarial drug.

Beginning in the 1960s, the People's Republic of China initiated an aggressive program to discover the scientific basis for many

◄ ROBERT BURNS WOODWARD (1917–1979) ►

A number of natural products have been found to be useful as drugs. One way to make those drugs available to humans is to harvest the natural products, extract the active ingredient, and make that ingredient available as a drug. That process is long and difficult, and it may often threaten the survival of the organism from which the drug is obtained. A far better approach is to determine the chemical structure of the active ingredient and then to find a way of making that chemical in the laboratory. Once a method for synthesizing the chemical has been determined, preparing the drug becomes a routine process of chemical production.

That approach sounds simple and direct. The problem is that the chemical component of many natural products is often very complex. A quick review of the chemical structures shown in this chapter confirms the challenge a chemist faces when he or she sets out to find a way of making a new product synthetically.

One of the great accomplishments in this field is represented by the work of Robert Burns Woodward in his elucidation of the structure of the quinine molecule in 1944. Quinine was, for centuries, the most important drug available for the treatment of malaria, a disease that affects hundreds of millions of people around the world. As a result of Woodward's work, it became possible to manufacture the drug synthetically rather than to collect it from its natural source, chinchona bark.

Robert Woodward was born in Boston on April 10, 1917. He graduated from Quincy High School, in Quincy, Massachusetts, in 1933, at the age of

traditional herbal remedies, including qing hoa. As a result of that program, in 1972 Chinese scientists identified the active ingredient in qing hoa, a substance they called qinghaosu. Qinghaosu is also known as arteannuin in China and as artemisinine in the West. Artemisinine is a sesquiterpene, a class of naturally occurring compounds with the general formula $C_{15}H_{24}$. The sesquiterpenes are considered to be chemically derived from the basic compound, isoprene. Chinese researchers have developed a number of derivatives of artemisinine, including the compounds known as artemether, artesunate, arteether and artelinate, all highly effective in the prevention and treatment of malaria. The structural

16. He entered the Massachusetts Institute of Technology the same year, where at first he did very poorly in his classes. He was bored by what he regarded as the slow pace of his instruction and would have left school had the chemistry faculty not recognized his genius in the subject. They arranged for him to design his own course of study and, now eager to pursue his own agenda, he graduated with a Ph.D. in chemistry only four years later, at the age of 20.

Woodward then moved across town in Cambridge to devote a year of postgraduate study at Harvard University. At the end of that year, he accepted an appointment to the Harvard chemistry faculty, a post he held for most of the rest of his life. One of his great interests at Harvard was the synthesis of large, complex molecules, the first of which was quinine in 1944. He followed that work with the elucidation of other molecular structures and the development of synthetic methods for each. Included among these molecules were penicillin (1945), patulin (1948), cholesterol and cortisone (1951), oxytetracycline (1952), strychnine (1954), lysergic acid (1954), reserpine (1956), chlorophyll (1960), colchicine (1963), cephalosporin C (1965), and vitamin B_{12} (1971).

Woodward was awarded the 1965 Nobel Prize in chemistry for his contributions in the field of chemical synthesis. He received many other awards also, including the Davy Medal (1959) and the Copley Medal (1978) of the Royal Society and the U.S. National Medal of Science (1964). He died of a heart attack in Cambridge on July 8, 1979.

formulas of artemisinine and its derivatives are shown in the following diagram. The formulas show the close structural relationship of the compounds, differing only in the shaded portion of the molecules.

The success in determining the chemical structure of qinghaosu is only one example of the accomplishments of chemists in attaining a better understanding of the relationship between the chemical structure of natural drugs and their pharmacological effects. Those accomplishments have formed the basis of a whole new phase of the pharmaceutical industry in which natural products and their derivatives provide an extensive source of new drugs.

Microorganisms as the Source of Drugs

Plants remained essentially the sole source of natural product drugs until well into the 20th century. Then in 1928 the discovery of penicillin by the Scottish bacteriologist Sir Alexander Fleming (1881–1955) opened an entirely new area of research in the field of

Chemical formulas for artemisinine and its derivatives

anti-infective drugs. Quite by accident, Fleming discovered that a sample of staphylococcus bacteria that he had inadvertently left out had begun to die out in certain areas of the culture. He determined that the change had come about in places where mold had fallen into the culture. Fleming isolated the mold and identified it as *Penicillium notatum*. He inferred that the mold produced some chemical with the ability to attack and kill bacteria, a chemical that he later isolated and named *penicillin*.

Penicillin was only the first of a new category of drugs that came to be called *antibiotics* (named by the Russian microbiologist Selman Waksman in 1941). Antibiotics were originally defined as chemical substances produced by microorganisms and able to inhibit the growth of or destroy bacteria and other microorganisms. It took more than a decade for the significance of Fleming's discovery to be appreciated and for penicillin to be adopted by the medical profession as a treatment for infectious diseases.

Once scientists turned that corner, however, they discovered a flood of new antibiotics in a relatively short period of time: streptomycin, by Waksman in 1943; bacitracin, by American bacteriologist Frank Meleney (1889–1963) in 1943; the cephalosporins, by Sardinian medical researcher Giuseppe Brotzu (1895–1976) in 1945; chloramphenicol, the first broad–range antibiotic, by the research team of John Ehrlich, Paul Burkholder and David Gotlieb, in 1947; chlortetracycline, by the American plant physiologist Benjamin Minge Duggar (1872–1956) in 1947; and neomycin by Waksman and his colleague Hubert Lechevalier in 1949.

Today, scientists have a good understanding of the molecular mechanisms antibiotic compounds use to impair or kill these disease-causing bacteria. In many instances, for example, an antibiotic molecule will bond with one of the enzymes responsible for the synthesis of a bacterial cell membrane. Openings develop in the cell membrane, water enters, and the cell bursts and dies. More than 150 different antibiotics are now available for treating a host of infectious diseases that had once been considered incurable, diseases such as plague, pneumonia, tuberculosis, typhus, typhoid fever, scarlet fever, staphylococcus infections, gonorrhea, meningitis, pertussis (whooping cough), and urinary tract infections. These antibiotics exist because researchers came to understand how certain microorganisms live and grow.

Marine Organisms as a Source of Drugs

People have long used marine organisms as the source of a limited number of synthetic products used in everyday life. Perhaps the most famous of these organisms has been the mollusk *Murex brandaris,* from which a beautiful purple dye can be extracted. The dye is obtained from a small organ of the mollusk (the hypobranchial gland), and its preparation is so expensive that it was traditionally used as a dye only for clothing worn by the nobility. For that reason, the dye was called *royal purple* or, more commonly, *Tyrian purple,* after the region from which it is obtained.

Traditionally, there has been almost no research into the use of marine organisms as a source of drugs. Beginning in the 1960s, however, that situation changed and people began to seek out and identify marine organisms that could be used as the source of natural-product-based drugs. One problem that has hindered research in this area is the difficulty of collecting and identifying marine organisms and of determining both the chemical products that can be extracted from them and the biological effects of those compounds. The 1990s saw a rapid growth of interest in this field of research, however, with almost half as many patents for marine products being granted from 1996 to 1999 as had been granted in the preceding 25 years.

At this point, only a handful of products derived from marine organisms have been approved by the FDA for sale to consumers. The majority of these products have been approved for nondrug use. For example, researchers at the University of California have extracted an anti-inflammatory agent, which they named *pseudopterosin,* from a Caribbean sea whip called *Pseudopterogorgia elisabethae.* Pseudopterosin is currently used as an additive to a cosmetic skin cream called Resilience® produced by Estée Lauder. Because the compound has undergone study only relatively recently, it is possible pseudopterosin will have important therapeutic applications, and researchers are exploring this possibility. For example, the compound is also being studied for possible use in the treatment of

© Infobase Publishing

Derivatives of pseudopterosin

various inflammatory disorders, such as rheumatoid arthritis, osteo-arthritis, rheumatic carditis, bronchial asthma, myasthenia gravis, and psoriasis. It is also being considered for use with insect bites and as additional treatment during organ and tissue transplants.

The diagram above shows how a large number of similar com-pounds can be produced by making changes in a basic molecule. In this diagram, R^1, R^2, and R^3 represent three positions in the ba-sic pseudopterosin molecule where atoms or groups of atoms can be added. If a hydrogen atom is used as a substituent at all three positions, the compound formed is called pseudopterosin A. If an acetate group is used at position R^1 and hydrogen atoms at R^2 and R^3, the compound is pseudopterosin B, and so on. Each compound in this family has generally similar characteristics but differs from its cousins' efficacy, chemical and physical properties, safety, and other properties.

Another commercially available product containing naturally occurring marine products is Formulaid®, produced by Martek Biosciences as a nutritional supplement for infant formulas. Formulaid® contains two fatty acids, arachidonic acid (ARA) and docosahexaenoic acid (DHA), extracted from a variety of marine microalgae. ARA and DHA are the most abundant polyunsaturated fatty acids found in breast milk, and they are the most important fatty acids used in the development of brain gray matter. They are especially desirable for use in infant formulas because they come from nonmeat sources and can be advertised as vegetarian additives to the product.

An especially intriguing pair of products obtained from marine organisms in recent years are Vent® and Deep Vent® DNA polymerase. These products are used in DNA research studies. Their special feature is that they are at least 10 times as efficient as other similar products in polymerase chain reactions because they can tolerate temperatures just below the boiling point of water, a characteristic that comparable research tools lack. Vent® and Deep Vent® DNA polymerases are obtained from the bacterium *Thermococcus litoralis,* which is found around deep-sea hydrothermal vents at the bottom of the ocean.

A number of other products obtained from marine organisms are used in research also. Among the best known of these is green fluorescent protein (GFP), a compound that fluoresces (gives off light when exposed to radiation) bright green when exposed to blue or ultraviolet light. When GFP is attached to a compound being studied in an experiment, the compound's movement can be followed visually because of the very noticeable green light produced by the GFP. Green fluorescent protein is obtained from a bioluminescent jellyfish, *Aequora victoria.*

Some scientists who study marine organisms believe that they may be at the threshold of an exciting new era in which extracts from such organisms can provide a host of new therapeutic drugs for use against some of the most intransigent diseases known to humans, including cancer and malaria. Two of the most promising of these products were discovered in the early 1950s by W. Bergmann, R. J. Feeney, and D. C. Burke. The products were modified forms of familiar nitrogen bases (aromatic carbon compounds that contain nitrogen) given the names of spongothymidine and spongouridine that demonstrated strong antitumor and antiviral properties. A synthetic analog of these natural products, arabinosyl cytosine, is now available commercially from the Pharmacia & Upjohn Company under the brand name of Cytosar-U®. As of this writing, it is the only marine-derived anticancer agent available for clinical use.

A number of other marine-derived products are waiting in the wings, however. Among the many compounds that have shown promise and are undergoing further testing for anticancer properties are halichondrin B, isolated from four marine sponge genera, *Halichondria, Axinella, Phakellia,* and *Lissodendoryx;* halomon, from the red alga *Portieria hornemannii;* dolastatin 10, from the sea slug (sea hare) *Dolabella auricularia;* and ecteinascidin 743, from the Caribbean sea squirt *Ecteinashidia turbinata.*

One of the compounds furthest along in development is bryostatin-1, derived from the marine bryozoan *Bugula neritina.* In 2001, the FDA granted *"orphan drug"* status to bryostatin-1, reserving marketing rights for the product to the German-based firm GPC Biotech AG. The compound has showed great promise for the treatment of esophageal cancer, especially when used in conjunction with another anticancer agent, Taxol®. It also appears to have potential value in the treatment of melanoma, ovarian cancer, and non-Hodgkin's lymphoma.

Drug researchers now hold high hopes for the promise of marine organisms as the source of new drugs. More than 80 percent of all life-forms on Earth exist only in the oceans, so a vast supply of organisms is available for study. Some authorities have stated that the chances of finding new drugs in marine organisms may be 300 to 400 times that of finding drugs in terrestrial organisms.

Plant Products as the Source of New Drugs

Despite all the contributions that microorganisms have made to the development of new drugs and all the promise held by marine organisms for such purposes, many researchers still count primarily on plants as the most likely source for the discovery of new drugs.

In some areas, that hope has already been realized. In 2002, authorities estimated that anywhere between one third and one-half of the best-selling prescription drugs used around the world were derived from natural products.

In recent years, however, some of the greatest emphasis has been placed on the search for anticancer and antiviral agents derived from natural products. Success in that area has not been as great as that achieved in other fields. Since 1960, only seven plant-derived drugs have been approved by the FDA for use as anticancer agents. Four of those drugs, vinblastine, vincristine, etoposide, and teniposide, were discovered in the 1950s. The last three—Taxol®, topotecan, and irinotecan—were discovered and approved much more recently.

The discovery of vinblastine and vincristine is one of the most intriguing examples of serendipity in scientific research in recent years. In 1952, the Canadian medical researcher Robert Laing Noble (1910–90) received a package from his brother, Dr. Clark Noble, containing 25 leaves from the Madagascar periwinkle plant, *Vinca rosea.* Clark had received the leaves from one of his patients in Jamaica, who said that natives on the island often used the plant to control their diabetes when insulin was not available. Clark, who was retired, suggested that his brother study the plant for possible use as a drug for the treatment of diabetes.

When Robert Noble carried out his studies on the periwinkle leaves, he found that they had no effect on blood sugar levels. However, they did appear to significantly reduce a subject's white blood cell count. Perhaps, Dr. Noble reasoned, the product could be used to treat diseases characterized by abnormally high white blood cell counts, such as leukemia. He was successful in isolating two chemicals from the periwinkle leaves, which he named vinblastine and vincristine, that markedly decreased white blood cell counts in patients with certain forms of cancer. The two chemicals were the first anticancer agents derived from natural sources to be approved for use with human patients.

Perhaps the most exciting story about an anticancer agent derived from a natural product is that of Taxol®. That story begins in 1958, when the National Cancer Institute began a program to screen natural products for substances that might have anticancer activity. The

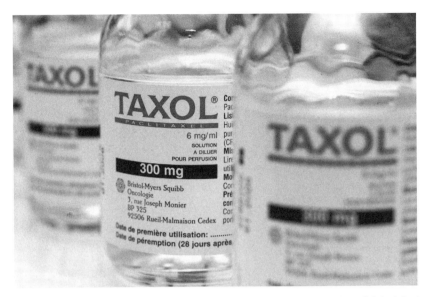

Taxol® is an anticancer drug obtained from the Pacific yew tree (*Taxux brevifolia*). (Alix/Phanie/Photo Researchers, Inc.)

plan was to examine more than 35,000 species in the research. Five years later, scientists at the Research Triangle Institute in North Carolina, Monroe Wall and M. C. Wani, found that the bark of the Pacific yew tree (*Taxux brevifolia*) demonstrated tumor-suppressing qualities. In 1971, those same scientists isolated a substance, which they called *compound 17,* responsible for this antitumor activity. Compound 17 was later renamed *paciltaxel.*

Hopes for using paciltaxel in the treatment of cancer were dampened, however, by the fact that the Pacific yew tree is a slow-growing, threatened tree. Its harvest for the collection of paciltaxel from its bark would almost certainly have led to the tree's extinction. Instead, researchers turned to the obvious alternative, characterization of the chemical structure of paciltaxel and its chemical synthesis. That task was a challenge, however, because of the complex structure of the paciltaxel molecule. After more than a decade of research, however, the task was accomplished: Researchers achieved a successful method for the synthesis of the compound in the laboratory. In 1992, the FDA approved paciltaxel for use against cancers that had failed to respond to other treatments. By this time, the compound was being made and marketed by Bristol-Myers Squibb Company under the trade name of Taxol®. Over the next decade, the FDA continued to expand the diseases for which Taxol® could be used, including breast, ovarian, and lung cancer and Kaposi's sarcoma related to HIV infection.

Another success story involving the development of anticancer agents is that of a drug known as *camptothecin*. The same researcher who had begun study of pacitaxel, Dr. M. E. Wall, first studied the natural product from which this drug was originally obtained, a tree native to China called *Camptotheca acuminata*, in the late 1950s. Although initial studies of its effects on tumors were encouraging, later tests were ambiguous, and interest in the

◄ MONROE WALL (1916–2002) AND MANSUKHLAL WANI (1925–) ►

Hopes were high in the 1960s that the next great breakthrough in pharmacology might be the discovery of natural products that were effective against cancer. The National Cancer Institute (NCI) sponsored an ambitious program to locate, collect, and analyze thousands of plant products that might have anticancer properties. The program was in existence only a short while before the first success was reported: Researchers discovered an extract from the bark of the Pacific yew tree (*Taxux brevifolia*) with anticancer properties. This discovery was made by the research team of Monroe E. Wall and Mansukhlal C. Wani at RTI (Research Triangle Institute) International, a research laboratory operated under the auspices of four universities, North Carolina State University, Duke University, the University of North Carolina at Charlotte, and North Carolina Central University.

Monroe Wall was born in Newark, New Jersey, on July 25, 1916. He attended grade and high school in East Orange, New Jersey, graduating in 1932. He then earned B.S. (1936), M.S. (1938), and Ph.D. (1939) degrees in agricultural biochemistry, all from Rutgers University.

From 1950 to 1960, Wall directed a research group at the Eastern Regional Research Laboratory (ERRL) of the U.S. Department of Agriculture at Wyndmoor, Pennsylvania. While at ERRL, Wall was in charge of NCI's first large-scale search for plants that might be used for the synthesis of corti-

drug waned until the mid-1980s. Then, however, efforts to make synthetic analogs of the natural product resulted in compounds that were at least as effective as the natural product itself—and safer. By 1985, the FDA had approved two compounds derived from camptothecin, *Hycamtin®* and *Camptostar®*, for use against ovarian and colon cancer. The discovery of pacitaxel and campto-thecin, the synthesis of their analogs, and their successes against certain forms of cancer have strongly encouraged the continued and expanded search for natural products that can be used against the dread disease.

The success of pacitaxel and camptothecin has motivated re-searchers to expand their search for other natural products with

sone and other steroid hormones. In 1958, he obtained an extract of the plant *Camptotheca acuminata* that demonstrated anticancer properties. In addition to his work on *Taxux brevifolia* and *Camptotheca acuminata*, Wall studied the synthesis and chemical properties of Δ-9-tetrahydrocannabinol (THC), the primary active ingredient in marijuana. In 1960, Wall moved to RTI, where he remained until his death on July 6, 2002. During this work, he developed the standard test now used to determine the presence of THC in urine. In recognition of his work, Rutgers University established the Monroe Wall Symposium, a biennial international scientific meeting about the search for pharmaceuticals from natural sources.

Mansukhlal Wani was born on February 20, 1925, in Nandurbar, Maharastra, India. He attended grade and high school in his hometown and then earned his bachelor's degree in chemistry (1947) and his master's degree in organic chemistry (1950) from the University of Bombay. He emigrated to the United States in 1958 and enrolled at Indiana University, from which he received his Ph.D. in chemistry in 1962. He accepted a position with RTI in 1962 and has remained with the organization ever since in the position of Principal Scientist.

Wall and Wani collaborated in their research on *Taxux brevifolia* and *Camptotheca acuminata* for 38 years. They have received some of the most prestigious awards given in their field of science, most notably the 2000 Charles F. Kettering Prize for outstanding research on the diagnosis or treat-ment of cancer.

anticancer and antiviral properties. In 2007, a number of products are at various stages of testing, including combretastatin A4, isolated from the South African medicinal tree, *Combretum caffrump;* homoharringtonine, from the tree *Cephalotaxus harringtonia* found in mainland China; ingenol 3-O-angelate, originally obtained from a common English and Australian tree *Euphorbia peplus;* and phenoxodiol, a synthetic analog of daidzein, obtained from soybean. This field of research obviously holds great promise for the development of new antiviral and anticancer drugs.

The Search for New Natural Product Drugs

Until the 1950s, the world approached the use of drugs to treat disease in either of two ways. Generally speaking, people living in developing nations relied primarily on natural products, especially herbs, to treat disease, while those living in developed nations put their faith in modern scientific medicine, usually synthetically produced chemical compounds, for the same purposes. The line between these two practices began to break down when scientific researchers started to search for the chemical compounds in natural products that are biologically active, research characterized by the work of Wall and Wani described in the previous section. In fact, the accomplishments of Wall and Wani prompted the National Cancer Institute (NCI) and the U.S. Department of Agriculture (USDA) to initiate a formal program for the collection and screening of plants with potential anticancer activity.

Between 1960 and 1982, that program was responsible for the collection of more than 35,000 plant samples, from which 114,000 unique extracts were obtained. In addition, field-workers collected 18,000 extracts from marine organisms. NCI and USDA terminated the program in 1982 because of limited success: Only seven plant-derived anticancer drugs had been developed as a result of the program, four resulting from Wall and Wani's 1950s research. NCI reactivated the program in 1986 as its Natural Products Branch (NPB), a division that remains in existence today. In 1988, the institute also began to search for drugs that might be effective against AIDS. Since its reactivation, NPB has screened more than 40,000 plant extracts. One of those, Taxol®, has been approved for use, and five others with potential use against AIDS have been isolated. Three of those are now in preclinical trials.

Researchers have adopted three approaches in their search for new drugs among natural products. First, they sometimes use a "broadcast" approach in which they simply collect and study all the plants or marine organisms within a certain geographical area. The advantage of this approach is that large numbers of samples can be collected in a relatively short time. The disadvantage is that there is seldom any particular reason for expecting to find a useful compound in any given area.

A second approach is to focus on plants or marine organisms that are known to contain biologically active compounds. The hope is that such plants or marine organisms may yield new and different chemicals that may also be effective against certain types of disease.

Finally, researchers may use an *ethnobotanical* approach, that is, one that focuses on medicinal plants that have traditionally been used in various cultures. The assumption underlying this approach is that plants on which people have relied for medicines in the past may very well contain biologically active chemicals that can be either isolated, purified, and used as drugs or used as models from which biologically active analogs can be produced.

Once a plant or marine organism sample has been collected, it is labeled, stored, and then treated chemically to remove its primary components. Next, these components (extracts) are tested to determine whether or not they show any biological activity. The tests (*bioassays*) are used to identify any toxicity or other effect an extract may have against target cells (such as cancer cells), organisms (such as parasites), or chemicals (such as allergens). Extracts that seem to be effective against any one of these targets are then analyzed in more detail to find out what chemical(s) they contain that produce the biological activity. When and if such compounds are identified, they are then subjected to the long and detailed series of tests for safety and efficacy that all new drugs undergo.

Natural Product Research and Biodiversity

Over the past few decades, the use of natural products as drugs and dietary supplements has raised an increasingly important question: What impact does it have on biodiversity? The widespread popularity of some natural products has resulted in their rapid destruction in the environment. One of the best-documented examples of this pattern is the decimation of wild echinacea resources throughout the United States. Sales of the plant in 2002 amounted to more than $32 million, and manufacturers are eager to obtain as much as they can from American sources. As a result, the plant is rapidly being depleted from its natural habitat, which ranges across large parts of the Midwest.

The popularity of ginseng has already led to its extinction in some parts of the world (such as South Korea) and to its classification as an endangered species in other parts (such as China) due to overharvesting. Today, more than 65 tons of the root are harvested in the United States each year, most of it going to the Far East. At this rate, the plant faces possible extinction in this country also.

Goldenseal is yet another threatened herb in the United States and other parts of the world. It currently sells for about $100 a pound, making it highly popular for individual, independent workers who tear it out of its natural habitat. In 2003, the Convention on International Trade in Endangered Species proposed listing it as an endangered species.

Such losses are potentially serious problems for drug research. Maintaining biodiversity is an essential component of future research efforts to identify possible drugs in the world's plant and marine resources. Scientists have no idea how many species there are in the world, but reasonable estimates place the numbers at about 250,000 plant species and up to 1 million marine species. So far, no more than about 10 percent of all plants and 1 percent of all marine organisms have been studied for possible use as drugs.

Given these circumstances, it is possible that countless numbers of new natural products with potential for use as drugs are still waiting to be discovered. As more and more plants and animals are destroyed each year by deforestation, development, and other forces, those natural products are being to lost for possible future use.

Natural Products as Dietary Supplements

Ask the average person on the street about "natural products," and he or she is likely to mention the kinds of products found on the shelves of grocery stores and stores that specialize in "organic" and "natural" foods. Those items are overwhelmingly plant products, and they range from aconitum napellus (monkshood), alfalfa, allium cepa, aloe vera, angelica, and anise seed to witch hazel, yarrow, yellow dock, yohimbe bark, and yucca.

Healers have used many of these products for centuries, and they remain widely popular with people in countries around the world today, both developed and developing. In many cultures,

---

◀ CLAIMS MADE FOR CERTAIN NATURAL PRODUCTS ▶

NATURAL PRODUCT	CLAIMED BENEFIT(S)
Echinacea	Stimulates immune system
Ginkgo (*Ginkgo biloba*)	Improves concentration and memory; protects against Alzheimer's disease
Ginseng (*Panax ginseng*)	Increases stamina and concentration
Glucosamine and chondroitin	Effective against arthritis and other joint diseases

(continues)

◁ **CLAIMS MADE FOR**
CERTAIN NATURAL PRODUCTS *(continued)* ▷

NATURAL PRODUCT	CLAIMED BENEFIT(S)
Hawthorn (*Crataegus sp.*)	Protects against heart disease
Kava (*Piper methysticum*)	Relieves nervousness and protects against stress
Ma huang (*Ephedra sinica*)	Protects against respiratory disorders
Saw palmetto (*Serenoa repens*)	Prevents prostate disease
St. John's wort (*Hypericum perforatum*)	Relieves anxiety and depression; prevents insomnia; relieves some skin disorders
Valerian (*Valeriana officinalis*)	Reduces nervousness and insomnia
Yohimbe bark	Improves sexual performance in males

Note: An FDA information sheet on claims that can be made for dietary supplements and foods can be found at http://vm.cfsan.fda.gov/~dms/hclaims.html.

---

they constitute the great majority of the pharmacopoeia of folk and traditional medicine.

Many people today believe that natural products are safer and at least as effective as synthetically produced medicines, such as antibiotics and anticancer agents. The variety of claims made for such products is very great, as shown in the chart above. The question is, however, how reliable are these claims?

In cultures where the scientific method is trusted and respected, the usual way to answer this question is with experimentation and tests. For example, a drug manufacturer that wishes to sell a new product in the United States must first go through a long, complex, and expensive testing process to show that the drug is safe for human use and effective against one or more health problems. That process typically takes many years (often more than 10) and costs many millions of dollars. A drug company that wanted to market a new plant product *as a drug* for use against asthma, for example, would have to go through just such a procedure to obtain permission from the FDA to market the drug.

The kind of natural products listed in the table above, however, are not defined in the United States today as *drugs* but as dietary supplements, nutritional supplements, natural foods, or some similar nondrug product. Such products are not subject to the same standards of testing as are synthetic drugs. They are regulated by the Dietary Supplement Health and Education Act (DSHEA) of 1994 (Public Law 103–417). According to that law, the makers of natural products used

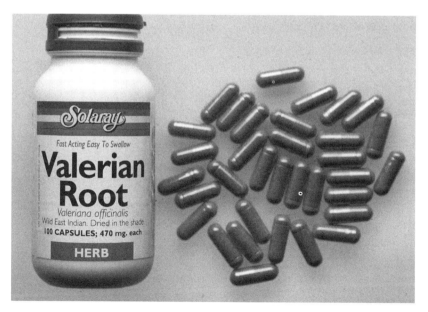

Valerian root pills are said to reduce insomnia and nervousness. (Will and Deni McIntyre/Photo Researchers, Inc.)

as dietary supplements do not have to prove that their products are either safe or effective; rather, it is the responsibility of the Food and Drug Administration to prove that any given supplement is harmful. If it should do so, it must then ask the Department of Health and Human Services to begin procedures to have the product removed from the marketplace.

The DSHEA allows manufacturers to make certain kinds of claims for their products (called *structure/function claims*), but not specific *health claims*. For example, a manufacturer can say that its product "supports the immune system," "promotes healthy joints," or "reduces stress." It cannot say that it "reduces the pain of arthritis," "improves the health of a person with a compromised immune system" (such as HIV infection), or "works as effectively as Prozac®." Manufacturers also have to include the following disclaimer on their labels and packages:

"This statement has not been evaluated by the Food and Drug Administration. This product is not intended to diagnose, treat, cure, or prevent any disease."

The benefits of the DSHEA to the manufacturers of natural products is obvious. They can claim a variety of health benefits for their products in very general terms that may sound to consumers like health claims but usually are not. They also *can* (although they are unlikely to attempt to) sell products that do not contain the chemicals listed on the label, are not safe for human consumption, or are not effective at treating the conditions for which they are recommended. In some ways, this situation sounds similar to the conditions that existed at the beginning of the 20th century, when the FDA was created to deal with the false and misleading claims of patent medicine suppliers.

On the other hand, some food companies have chosen to pursue the steps necessary to obtain FDA approval for certain specific health claims for their natural food products. For example, the Kellogg company received approval in 1998 to say that the soluble fiber obtained from psyllium seed husks can help reduce coronary heart disease. General Mills received FDA permission a year later to make a similar claim for its whole-grain cereal products. At this point in time, however, there is little or no scientific evidence to support the kinds of claims made for most natural products like those in the table above.

The lack of such scientific evidence does not automatically mean that such products are dangerous or ineffective. Many people are willing to trust traditional practices that have been used for hundreds of years whether there is scientific evidence for them or not. They are willing to accept the claims of healers from fields other than modern medicine about the benefits of such products. Indeed, an important reason for the adoption of the DSHEA in 1994 was to allow individuals the right to make choices about dietary supplements without the intervention of the federal government in that process.

Section 13 of the Dietary Supplement Health and Education Act of 1994 created an Office of Dietary Supplements as part of the National Institutes of Health. The office was given two primary responsibilities: (1) to explore more fully the potential role of dietary supplements as a significant part of the efforts of the United States to improve health care; and (2) to promote scientific study of the benefits of dietary supplements in maintaining health and preventing chronic disease and other health-related conditions.

Since the office was established, it has collected evidence and supported research to determine the safety and effectiveness of dietary supplements. Given the large number of dietary supplements currently available and the difficulty of collecting complete evidence, the Office has so far released a relatively limited amount of information about the safety and effectiveness of dietary supplements. A few of its initial findings are summarized in the table below.

The use of natural products as drugs among some people remains as popular today as it has for centuries in spite of considerable uncertainty as to the efficacy and, in some cases, the safety of such chemicals. Researchers continue to explore the mechanisms by which such chemicals work, their effectiveness in combating certain diseases, and the possibilities of developing analogs that may be both more effective and safer for use in treating human diseases.

◀ **CURRENT INFORMATION ON
CERTAIN DIETARY SUPPLEMENTS** ▷

DIETARY SUPPLEMENT	CURRENT INFORMATION
Black cohosh	Preliminary evidence for effective use against "hot flashes" and other menstrual problems
Coenzyme Q_{10}	Stimulates immune system; protects against certain heart disorders
Garlic products	No reduction in risk for breast, lung, gastric, colon, or rectal cancer when used for less than three to five years; no evidence on protection from heart disease; some evidence for limited protection against laryngeal, gastric, colorectal, and endometrial cancers
Green tea	Early, limited, and contradictory studies suggest some protection against certain types of cancer
Milk thistle	Ambiguous and uncertain evidence for protection against liver disorders
St. John's wort	Possibly effective against mild to moderate depression; no evidence for its effectiveness against moderate to severe depression
Thunder god vine	One study shows some relief from symptoms of rheumatoid arthritis

Further information on the safety and efficacy of natural products is available on the Office's Web site at http://ods.od.nih.gov/index.aspx and from a number of other sources, one of the best of which is the "Natural Products" page maintained by Solumedia at http://www.solumedia.com/nature.htm.

The Safety of Natural Products as Drugs

Natural products that have been certified for use as drugs by the FDA are almost certainly safe and effective. They have gone through extensive tests that guarantee that they will not kill humans or cause any serious diseases. They have also been demonstrated to produce the medical benefits claimed for them.

As already discussed, the same cannot be said for natural products used as dietary supplements. In most cases, those drugs have not been subjected to the programs of testing required for FDA approval. As a result, products may pose a hazard to human health. Those hazards usually fall into one of four categories: (1) the product may prevent a person from receiving other forms of FDA-approved medication that may be more beneficial to them; (2) it may interact with other herbal medicines, prescribed drugs, and over-the-counter medications, with harmful effects; (3) it may have no effect at all on a person's health or well-being; or (4) it may actually cause harm to a person's health.

In the first instance, individuals seeking treatment for a disease or other health problem often have an opportunity to choose between drugs prescribed by a medical doctor and natural products, perhaps based on the advice of other healers, that they believe will cure the problem. A person generally bases this decision simply on the way he or she views the world and the causes of health and disease. In some cultures, for example, people believe, on the basis of their own cultural norms, that religious charms, shaman rites, natural products, or other nonscientific approaches are legitimate ways to treat disease. They trust centuries of tradition to provide them with the guidance they need to achieve good health.

In other cultures, many people believe that treatments for disease should be subjected to and based on scientific experimentation. Such individuals rely only on drugs and medical treatments that have undergone rigorous tests and demonstrated both safety and efficacy.

In free societies, individuals are able to choose between one approach or the other to the treatment of disease. The risk is that a person may choose one form of treatment (such as herbal medicine, for example) when a more efficacious medical treatment is available that could save his or her life. Obviously, the reverse is also true, at least in theory. A person might choose to follow a scientific regimen of treatment that involves the use of synthetic drugs, which always *might* have harmful side effects, when he or she might have been cured, or at least not harmed, by taking herbal medicines.

As more and more people rely on dietary supplements, the incidence of the second problem, harmful interactions, increases. That is, many individuals today take both prescription or over-the-counter FDA medicines *and* dietary supplements. What is the risk that two or more of these products will interact with each other, producing unexpected medical problems?

That question is now the subject of extensive research, and a number of findings have been reported in the last decade. Some examples of those findings include the following:

➢ Glucosamine (used to treat joint problems) can raise blood sugar levels, creating problems for diabetics.

➢ In people who take the protease inhibitor indinavir, the herb St. John's wort reduces the concentration of indinavir in the blood. A similar interaction has been reported between St. John's wort and the heart medication digoxin.

➢ The dietary supplement kava has been found to interact with alprazolam, a drug used to treat anxiety.

➢ In some individuals, ginkgo and aspirin interact to reduce the production of platelets, particles that are essential in the formation of blood clots, increasing the severity of bruising and bleeding.

➢ Ginseng interacts with phenelzine, a drug used to treat depression, stimulating the central nervous system.

➢ Anticoagulants (drugs that prevent blood from clotting), such as nonsteroidal anti-inflammatory drugs, aspirin, and heparin, interact with a number of natural products to increase the potential for bleeding. Among these products are chamomile, fish oil (omega-3 fatty acids), vitamin E, ginger, and goldenseal.

➤ Echinacea acts to decrease the effectiveness of certain immunodepressant agents, such as cyclosporine, azathioprine, and tacrolimus.

➤ Valerian, ginger, goldenseal, and chamomile all interact with sedatives (such as barbiturates and alcohol) to increase sedative effects.

These findings do not suggest that every drug interaction listed will result in a fatality or a traumatic effect on a person's health. The risk involved in taking aspirin and fish oil supplements, for example, is probably very low for most people. Some of these drug interactions, however, are more potent than others, and some individuals are more likely to be susceptible to such interactions than others. The lessons to be learned from this list of findings are that users should be aware of potential risks of taking various combinations of drugs; they should inform their doctors of such combinations; and they must be alert for symptoms of such interactions.

A third potential hazard of taking dietary supplements, that they may have no effect at all on one's health, is perhaps more benign. As discussed earlier in this chapter, the manufacturers of supplements are not required to demonstrate that they are effective for the conditions for which they are advertised and sold. Many people who use dietary supplements are aware of this problem and are willing to take a chance that the product *may* be effective in their own individual case. As some people argue, they simply do not have anything to lose by trying the product (as long as it does not produce interactions with other medications and is not, itself, actually harmful).

The fourth safety concern in the use of dietary supplements, that they may actually be harmful to users, is anything but benign. Recall that the DSHEA places the responsibility for safety testing with supplement manufacturers themselves. Consumers can only assume that products they purchase are safe for their use and will not cause health problems. It is only when such problems actually arise and the FDA is notified that regulators can deal with the safety of a supplement.

Experience over the past few decades has shown that some dietary supplements are, in fact, *not* safe and that in some cases they may pose very serious health threats to humans. Some examples are the following:

> In 1989, the amino acid dietary supplement L-tryptophan was thought to be associated with an outbreak of eosinophila-myalgia syndrome (EMS), a condition characterized by an increase in white blood cell count, severe muscle pain, and other skin and neuromuscular problems. Later studies showed that an impurity present during the manufacture of the amino acid was probably responsible for the outbreak of EMS and that the amino acid itself was probably safe for human consumption.

> Some athletes take the supplement called yohimbine because it increases muscle mass. There is some evidence, however, that the product causes problems ranging from headache and anxiety to high blood pressure, heart palpitations, elevated heart rate, and hallucinations.

> In 2002, the FDA issued a consumer advisory warning about kava (*Piper methysticum*), a plant indigenous to the South Pacific, stating that severe liver damage could be associated with the ingestion of products containing kava. The FDA had received reports of more than 25 cases of liver damage associated with the product, four of which required liver transplants.

> The FDA issued a consumer advisory in 2001 about the dietary supplement comfrey (*Symphytum officionale, Symphytum asperum,* and *Symphytum x. uplandicum*), sometimes recommended for digestive problems, because the product may be associated with liver disease.

> In 2001, the FDA found that a number of botanical products brought to its attention contained aristolochic acid, a chemical that has been implicated in kidney disease. The agency advised consumers to discontinue the use of any supplement that contained this chemical.

One of the dietary supplements that has raised the most safety concerns in recent years is ephedra. Ephedra is an extract from a plant known as *ma huang,* reputedly used by Chinese practitioners for more than 5,000 years to treat asthma and upper respiratory infections. It is known by a variety of other names, including Mormon tea, squaw tea, and herbal ecstasy. In recent years, ephedra has been promoted by manufacturers of the product as a tool for weight loss, enhanced sports performance, and increased energy.

By early 2003, however, the FDA had received 16,000 reports of "adverse events" apparently related to use of the product. Among these events were two deaths, four heart attacks, nine strokes, one seizure, and five psychiatric events for which no explanation other than use of the product could be found. Although ephedra accounts for less than 1 percent of all sales of dietary supplements, it accounts for 64 percent of all adverse events reported to the FDA. The agency's decision to take action against ephedra may have been influenced by the death of 23-year-old Baltimore Orioles pitcher Steve Bechler on February 19, 2003, a tragedy attributed to the baseball player's use of ephedra.

The principal active ingredient in ephedra is ephedrine. Synthetically produced ephedrine has been approved by the FDA for use as a drug. Under those more controlled conditions, the compound has not been associated with any adverse events of the kind reported for the natural product.

In the decade following the 1994 adoption of the DSHEA, a number of problems related to the manufacture, advertising, and sale of dietary supplements had become apparent. Findings accumulated that such products are often contaminated with a variety of impurities, such as bacteria, glass, lead, and pesticides. For example:

➤ One company withdrew a niacin product it marketed because capsules contained 10 times the quantity of niacin claimed. Users experienced heart attacks, nausea and vomiting, and liver damage as a result of using the product.

➤ Five out of 18 products containing soy or red clover were found to have as little as half the amount of isoflavone, the natural product they were designed to deliver, claimed on the label.

➤ One brand of folic acid, recommended for pregnant women, contained about a third of the vitamin claimed on the product label.

> A bee extract was found to have been contaminated with lead.

> Of 12 different bodybuilding supplements tested, only one contained the amount of the hormone androstenedione listed on the product label.

In early 2003, the FDA proposed new regulations designed to deal with two ongoing issues: contamination of such products and fraudulent practices used in their marketing. The new regulations required manufacturers to ensure that the products they sold were pure and free of dangerous contaminants and to ensure that they actually contained the chemicals listed on labels.

Many consumer advocates applauded the FDA for its efforts to impose new regulations on dietary supplements. Even the adoption of these regulations, however, would not guarantee that such products, *in and of themselves,* are either safe or effective.

As has been the case for centuries, many people continue to rely on natural products for the treatment of a host of physical and mental problems ranging from the common cold and rashes to cancer and loss of memory. Scientific evidence for the efficacy of many of these products is weak, but users accept cultural, historical, religious, quasi-medical, and other justifications for their use. The sale of dietary supplements in the United States alone nearly doubled in less than a decade, growing from $8.8 billion in 1994 to an estimated $15.7 billion in 2000. Clearly, whatever disadvantages they may have in terms of efficacy and safety, natural products will continue to constitute a major portion of the drug market in the United States and other countries around the world.

At the same time, researchers remain interested in learning more about the mechanisms by which some natural products exert their effects on the human body and chemical changes that can be made to produce more effective drugs. They also continue their search in the natural world for plants, marine organisms, and other materials that hold promise for possible medicinal uses in the treatment of a wide range of diseases and disorders.

3
RECOMBINANT DNA AS A NEW SOURCE OF DRUGS

It was August 1933. Eleven-year-old Emma had not been feeling well for some time. She seemed to be very thirsty and hungry much of the time. She also found that she had to make many more trips to the bathroom than usual, especially at night. And she felt very tired much of the time, quite a change for a girl who had always been active and eager to play. When she started to lose weight for no apparent reason, Emma's parents decided it was time for her to see a doctor. The doctor's prognosis was very frightening for Emma and her parents: She had diabetes.

Diabetes is a medical condition that develops when a person's body is unable to metabolize glucose ("blood sugar") properly. The glucose accumulates in the body and may damage the heart, kidneys, eyes, and nervous system. Left untreated, diabetes can lead to very serious health problems, including coma and death. Diabetes is currently the sixth most common cause of death in the United States.

When Emma received her doctor's diagnosis, only one effective treatment for diabetes was available: daily injection of extracts taken from the pancreases of a cow or pig. These extracts contained animal insulin that was enough like human insulin to metabolize glucose, a task that a diabetic's own body is unable to carry out. Preparing these extracts, however, was very time-consuming and expensive, and there were never enough cow and pig pancreases available to meet the needs of every diabetic in the United States, even though every pancreas available from slaughterhouses throughout the country was used to make animal insulin for human diabetics.

Had this situation not changed, untold numbers of diabetics would have died or suffered serious health problems because of the shortage of animal insulin for their treatment. Fortunately, an important scientific breakthrough made possible the production of insulin from another source: recombinant DNA. Today, human insulin can be made synthetically by means of recombinant DNA, assuring that every diabetic in the country will have an adequate supply of the hormone they need to stay alive and remain healthy.

Principles of Recombinant DNA

The term *recombinant DNA* refers to any DNA molecule that has been produced by joining genetic material from two different sources. The term is also used to describe the process by which this type of DNA is produced. That process usually involves the insertion of a gene from one organism into the genome of a different organism, usually that of a different species. For example, a human gene might be inserted into bacterial DNA, forming a new, mixed kind of bacterial DNA sometimes called *chimeric DNA.* That name comes from the mythical Greek monster called the *chimera,* which had the head of a lion, the body of a goat, and the tail of a serpent.

Recombinant DNA is a form of *genetic engineering,* the process by which a molecule of DNA has been artificially altered by any means whatsoever. Recombinant DNA and genetic engineering are both forms of an even more general process known as *biotechnology.* Biotechnology has been defined in a number of ways. The definition adopted by the Convention on Biological Diversity, an important international agreement, is "any technological application that uses biological systems, living organisms, or derivatives thereof, to make or modify products or processes for specific use."

DNA (the acronym for deoxyribonucleic acid) is a large molecule having roughly the shape of two spaghetti strands wrapped around each other. The chemical structures for the three kinds of chemical units found in DNA are shown below. These units are a sugar (de-

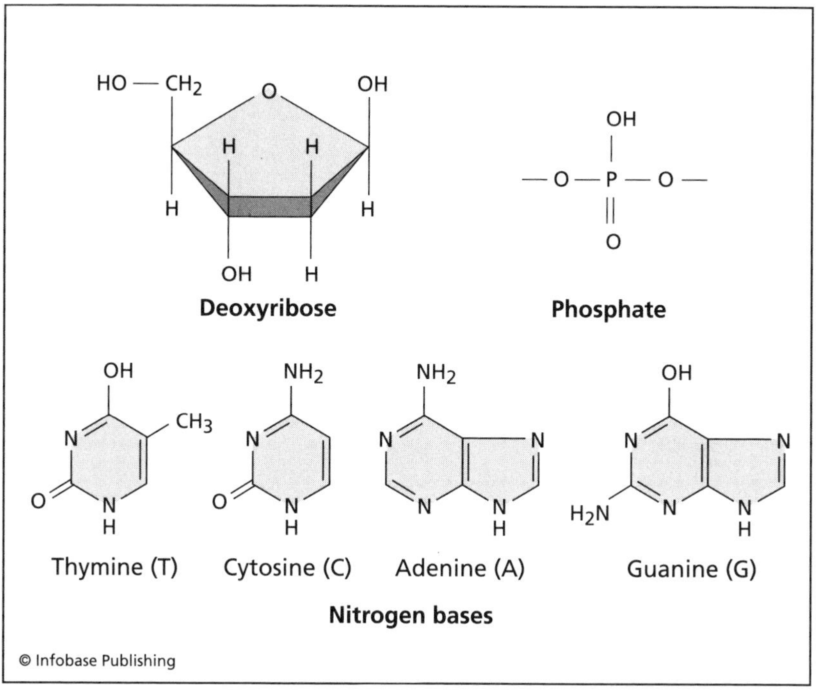

HO — CH₂ O OH

H H

H H

OH H

Deoxyribose

OH

— O — P — O —

O

Phosphate

OH NH₂ NH₂ OH

CH₃

N N N N N N

O N O N N N N N

H H H H₂N N H

Thymine (T) Cytosine (C) Adenine (A) Guanine (G)

Nitrogen bases

© Infobase Publishing

The three chemical units that make up DNA

oxyribose), a phosphate group, and four nitrogen bases: adenine, cytosine, guanine, or thymine. The four bases are usually represented by capital letters: A, C, G, and T, respectively.

The backbone of the DNA molecule is a chain of sugar and phosphate molecules, as shown in the diagram below. Attached to each sugar unit in the chain is one of the four nitrogen bases. The combination of a sugar unit bonded to a nitrogen base is called a *nucleoside.* The three-membered unit consisting of a sugar, phosphate group, and nitrogen base is known as a *nucleotide.*

A complete DNA molecule is a *dimer,* a molecule that consists of two similar units called monomers. Those units are extended strands of nucleotides joined to each other in a shape somewhat like that of a ladder. The two strands that make up a DNA molecule in turn are held together loosely by hydrogen bonds between adjacent nitrogen bases on opposite DNA strands.

Backbone of the DNA molecule

The DNA dimer has a three-dimensional form, produced when the two strands twist around each other in a form known as an α-*helix* (alpha-helix), like that shown in the diagram on page 57.

DNA is the "mastermind" of a living cell. It carries the instructions that supervise all of the biochemical changes that take place during growth, development, differentiation, metabolism, and other processes that take place in cells. It also carries the genetic information that organisms pass on to their progeny during the process of reproduction. DNA directs such changes by forming a second type of nucleic acid molecule called *ribonucleic acid* (or RNA), which, in turn, directs the synthesis of all the proteins needed by cells. In brief, this process can be represented as follows:

$$DNA \rightarrow RNA \rightarrow proteins$$

The mechanism by which this process occurs is, considering its importance to a living organism, remarkably simple. The key to DNA's ability to carry and transmit a genetic message is the sequence of nitrogen bases. Each set of three nitrogen bases (called a *triad*) in its molecule represents a code for the synthesis of a specific amino acid (hence, it is also called a *codon*). Suppose, for example, that a section of DNA contains the following sequence of nitrogen bases:

- A - T - T - C - G - G - C - A - C - A - G - C -

The first set of three nitrogen bases in this sequence, - A - T - T -, codes for the amino acid isoleucine. The second set of bases,

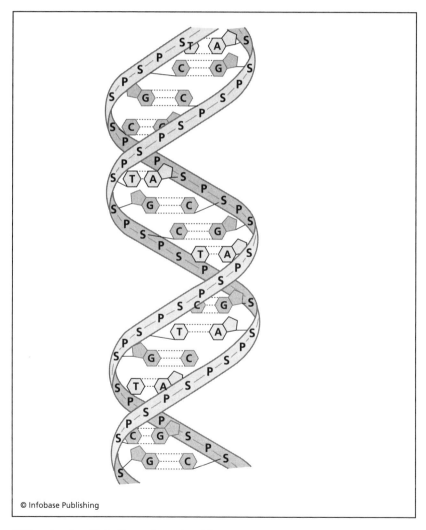

© Infobase Publishing

DNA molecule with its three-dimensional form

◁ PAUL BERG (1926–) ▷

"Community" and "cooperation" are key words associated with much of the scientific research that takes place today. When Celera Genomics announced the results of its human genome sequencing project in February 2001, 250 individuals from 24 different institutions and organizations were listed as authors of the paper published in the journal *Nature*. While the size of that collaboration was unusual, the fact that the discovery was the product of a group project is not. Many important scientific discoveries are the result of such team efforts. It is rather striking, then, that one can point to a single individual in the field of recombinant DNA research and say, "That person started it all." Without stretching history too much, that can be said of Paul Berg.

During the late 1960s, Berg was an associate professor at Stanford University School of Medicine, where he was attempting to work out the molecular dynamics of carcinogenesis, the process by which cancers originate and develop. Berg had chosen to work with a virus that causes tumors in monkeys, called SV40 (for simian virus 40). After determining the molecular sequence of the genes in SV40, Berg decided to try inserting genes from SV40 into a common bacterium, *Escherichia coli* (*E. coli*).

The method he developed for doing so is now the basic procedure used in recombinant DNA research. First, he used *restriction enzymes* to slice open SV40 DNA and remove genes from the virus's DNA. Then, using ligases, he inserted viral genes into the DNA of a bacteriophage (a virus that infects bacteria). The final step in the experiment would have been to insert the chimeric DNA into the bacterium. It was a step, however, that Berg never carried out. He was concerned that the new *transgenic organism* might somehow escape from the laboratory and spread SV40 genes to humans. In recognition of Berg's development of this extraordinary technique, he was awarded a share of the 1980 Nobel Prize in chemistry.

Paul Berg was born in Brooklyn, New York, on June 30, 1926. He attended Abraham Lincoln High School, from which he graduated in 1943. He then entered Pennsylvania State University (PSU), from which he earned a degree in biochemistry in 1948. His college career was interrupted from 1943 to 1946 while he served in the U.S. Navy. After receiving his B.S. from PSU, Berg enrolled at Western Reserve University (now Case Western Reserve University) to continue his studies in biochemistry. He received his Ph.D. in 1952, after which he spent one year as an American Cancer Society research fellow at the Institute of Cytophysiology in Copenhagen. He then took a position in biochemistry at Washington University in St. Louis, where he served until 1959. Berg then accepted an appointment at Stanford, an affiliation he has maintained to the present day.

At Stanford, Berg has been Willson Professor of Biochemistry, chairman of the Department of Biochemistry, Fellow of the Salk Institute, Robert W. and Vivian K. Cahill Professor of Cancer Research, Emeritus, and director and director emeritus of the Beckman Center for Molecular and Genetic Medicine. The focus of much Berg's research in the last three decades has been the mechanisms by which cells repair damage to their DNA.

Berg is known in the scientific community not only for his discoveries but also for his concern about the possible social consequences that such discoveries may have. In 1974, shortly after completing the first recombinant DNA experiments, Berg wrote a letter to the journal *Science,* warning of the risks transgenic organisms posed if they escaped from the laboratories in which they were produced. "New DNA elements introduced into *E. coli,*" he wrote, "might possibly become widely disseminated among human, bacterial, plant, or animal populations with unpredictable effects."

Berg went on to suggest that a protocol (set of rules) be developed to control the kinds of research that could be done on transgenic organisms and the conditions under which that research should take place. Berg's letter later became the basis for a federal voluntary policy on recombinant research that was developed at a famous conference held in 1975 at the Asilomar Conference Center in Pacific Grove, California.

Ironically, two of the cosigners of Berg's 1974 letter to *Science* and fellow attendees at the Asilomar conference, Herbert Boyer and Stanley Cohen, took the important next step in recombinant DNA research shortly after Berg announced his breakthrough. They took the final step that Berg had disavowed, namely the insertion of chimeric DNA into a living cell, the *E. coli* bacterium. Boyer and Cohen showed not only that the DNA of two organisms could be combined but that the transgenic organism produced could survive and reproduce.

In the eighth decade of his life, Berg remains active both as a researcher and as an advocate for the scientific community at the state and federal levels. In addition to serving as chair of the scientific advisory committee of the Human Genome Project, he has spoken and written in support of federal and state financing for stem cell research, human cloning, and other forms of biotechnology.

- C - G - G -, codes for the amino acid arginine. The third set of bases, - C - A - C -, codes for the amino acid histidine, and so on.

In this manner, the DNA strand shown above would direct the synthesis of a strand of RNA that would, in turn, direct the synthesis of a protein molecule. The protein molecule in the example given would consist of an isoleucine molecule (-A-T-T-) attached to an arginine molecule (-C-G-G-), attached to a histidine molecule (-C-A-C-), and so on: Ile-Arg-His- . . . . The molecule formed in this way might be the enzyme needed by cells to assist in the breakdown of glucose molecules, to form red blood cells, to build cell walls, or to carry out some other essential function in cells.

A strand of DNA, then, carries all the directions needed for the production of a specific protein. In biological terms, that strand of DNA is a gene. The term *gene* has a variety of definitions. Biologically, it is a unit of inheritance or a determinant of a phenotype (the observable characteristics of an individual). Chemically, a gene is a sequence of nitrogen bases that directs the formation of a specific protein. These separate definitions call attention to the fact that there are two different "languages" for talking about biological materials and processes: a biological language and a chemical language. At one time, biologists knew that hereditary traits are transmitted from one generation to the next by means of some kind of genetic "unit" that they called the *gene*. Until the mid-1950s, no one really knew what a "gene" was, other than some material that was passed down from cells of a parent to cells of its offspring.

In the 1950s, scientists discovered that this hereditary unit was actually a portion of a DNA molecule, a set of nucleotides or nitrogen bases that codes for various types of genetic information. Today, remnants of both languages remain in discussions of the ways cells work and the way genetic information is transmitted. In fact, a gene is both a unit of inheritance that determines the development of a particular phenotype *and* a portion of a DNA molecule that contains some specific sequence of nitrogen bases.

How does all this relate to recombinant DNA? The key is that it often takes a change of only one nitrogen base in a gene to completely alter both the RNA molecule formed and, hence, the protein molecule it synthesizes in a cell. Returning to the earlier example, suppose that the very first nitrogen base in the sequence were changed from "A" to "T," as follows:

-T-T-T-C-G-G-C-A-C-A-G-C-

The first triad in this sequence, - T - T - T-, codes not for isoleucine, but for phenylalanine, a different amino acid. The protein formed from this gene would be different from that formed by the sequence in the original DNA sequence. It would have the structure Phe-Arg-His- . . . rather than Ile-Arg-His- . . . , and, in all likelihood, it would perform an entirely different function in cells. This means that by manipulating a small fragment of genetic material, a scientist can change the genetic message and potentially generate desired biological compounds.

The Process of Recombinant DNA

As explained in the preceding section, DNA lends itself to recombination by virtue of its structure, but how is recombinant DNA carried out in practice in the production of drugs?

This researcher is growing recombinant bacteria that will produce a compound to be tested as a drug for HIV infection. (David Parker/Photo Researchers, Inc.)

Suppose, for example, the goal is to create an organism that is capable of producing human insulin. That organism could be a bacterium, a cow, a pig, a sheep, or any other nonhuman organism that carries a gene with the ability to synthesize human insulin. Such an organism would be called a *transgenic* organism because it contains one or more genes from some other kind of organism: a bacterium with a human gene for insulin, a cow with a human gene for insulin, a pig with a human gene for insulin, and so on.

Recombinant DNA is a process of a few important steps. The first step in that process is to locate a gene (often called an *oligonucleotide*) that codes for the protein one wishes to produce. In general, there are two ways to obtain a desired gene: (1) by extracting it from a cell or (2) by synthesizing it chemically.

Once the desired gene (such as the one that directs the synthesis of human insulin) has been located, some mechanism must be found for inserting it into the host animal (the bacterium, cow, pig,

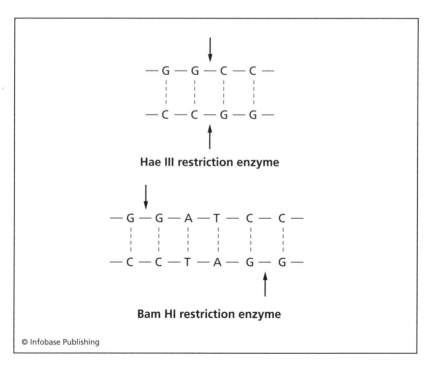

© Infobase Publishing

Cuts made by HaeIII restriction enzyme and by BamH I restriction enzyme

or sheep). The "carrier" of that gene into the host is called a *vector*. Before inserting the vector into the host organism, the gene must be attached to the vector. A vector is usually a virus or a special type of bacterial DNA called a *plasmid*. A plasmid is different from a DNA molecule in that it is, first, much smaller than such molecules, usually containing only a few genes, and, second, its shape is circular, rather than linear.

DNA molecules, whether linear or circular, can be cut by means of enzymes known as *restriction enzymes*. A restriction enzyme is an enzyme that recognizes certain sequences of nitrogen bases and breaks the bonds at some point within that sequence. Since these enzymes work on bonds within the DNA molecule, they are sometimes called *restriction endonucleases*.

Well over a hundred restriction enzymes are known. Each one recognizes and cuts a specific nitrogen base sequence. For example, the enzyme known as HaeIII (for the bacterium *Hemophilus aegypticus*) recognizes the sequence on page 62 and cuts the sequence between the G and C, as indicated by the arrows in this diagram. The "cuts" formed by HaeIII go cleanly through the DNA, forming "blunt" ends.

By contrast, other restriction enzymes cut at different portions of a DNA molecule, forming an "offset" break with "sticky" ends. For example, the restriction enzyme known as BamHI cuts between two GG nitrogen bases, but at different parts of the DNA molecule, forming "overhangs" or sticky ends. These sticky ends provide locations at which new nitrogen base sequences can be inserted.

Once the plasmid DNA has been opened by a restriction enzyme, the desired oligonucleotide is added, along with another type of enzyme, known as a *ligase*. Ligases are enzymes that catalyze the formation of covalent bonds. In the recombinant DNA process, the ligase promotes the formation of bonds between the sticky ends of the plasmid and the oligonucleotide that has been added. The result of this process is a new, chimeric DNA that consists primarily of the plasmid DNA but now contains the gene coding for the desired property.

Finally, the chimeric DNA is reinserted into a host cell, such as a bacterium. If the procedure is carried out properly, the chimeric DNA begins to function just as it would in any bacterial cell. The bacterial genes it contains continue to function as they normally

◄ WERNER ARBER (1929–   ) ►

One perhaps should be forgiven for thinking of bacteria and other one-celled organisms as "simple." They certainly are not very complex, compared with multicellular organisms such as a cabbage, a pet cat, or a favorite chemistry teacher. Yet bacteria are surprisingly complex chemical systems, with many of the same capabilities available to their more complex cousins in the animal world. This complexity arises at least in part because of the amazing flexibility and "imagination" of the DNA found in their cells.

For example, imagine that the DNA in a bacterium is damaged in some way—It may have been struck by an errant X-ray, for example. Without an intact, functioning DNA molecule, the bacterial cell will be unable to carry out its normal functions in the cell, and the bacterium may die. But evolution has developed a way of solving such problems. It has made available to the bacterial DNA certain kinds of enzymes—called *ligases*—whose job it is to search out and repair damaged sections of DNA.

Restriction enzymes are another lifesaving mechanism that bacteria have evolved for their survival. Restriction enzymes can be considered a part of a bacterium's immune system, a system that is called its restriction-modification (or RM) system. This system was first discovered and explained by the Swiss microbiologist Werner Arber in 1968.

Arber's work was inspired by an earlier discovery of the famous Italian-American microbiologist Salvador Luria (1912–1991). In 1942, Luria discovered that bacteria, like humans, seem to have mechanisms for protecting themselves from attacking viruses. Viruses that infect bacteria have a special name: bacteriophages. Arber discovered that this defensive system consisted of two parts: (1) a group of enzymes (restriction enzymes) that

would, and the inserted gene also begins to function, producing the protein for which it was designed.

Drugs Produced by Recombinant DNA

Over the past three decades, recombinant DNA research has resulted in the production of dozens of new drugs, of which the U.S. Food and Drug Administration (FDA) has approved about 50 for general use. These drugs include insulin (for the treatment of dia-

were able to cut apart the attacking virus's DNA and (2) a second group of enzymes (methylases) that modified the virus's DNA by attaching methyl groups (-CH3) to certain nitrogen bases in the DNA. Arber's discovery provided not only an important key in understanding the nature of bacteria but also an important tool that could be used in recombinant DNA research and other types of DNA modification studies. For his discovery of the bacterial RM system, Arber was awarded a share of the 1978 Nobel Prize for physiology or medicine.

Werner Arber was born in Gränichen, Switzerland, on June 3, 1929. He attended public schools in Gränichen and the Kantonssschule Aarau ("county high school") before enrolling at the Swiss Polytechnic School in Zürich. He received his degree in biology there in 1953 and then moved on to the University of Geneva, where he served as a research assistant while pursuing graduate studies in the field of biophysics. It was during this period that Arber learned about the work of Italian-American biologist Salvador Luria with bacteriophages and became interested in learning more about these viral particles. He completed his Ph.D. studies on this topic and received his degree from Geneva in 1958.

After a two-year program of postdoctoral studies at the University of Southern California, Arber returned to Geneva, where he completed the research that led to his understanding of bacterial RM. He remained at Geneva until 1970, when he resigned to spend a year as visiting professor in the Department of Molecular Biology at the University of California at Berkeley. He then returned to Switzerland and accepted an appointment as professor of molecular biology at the University of Basel, where he remained until 1996. He continues to carry out research at the university's Biozentrum research center as emeritus professor of molecular microbiology.

betes), alpha interferon (an anticancer agent), a vaccine for hepatitis B, granulocyte-macrophage colony-stimulating factor (GMCSF; used in the treatment of people with damaged immune systems), granulocyte-colony stimulating factor (G-CSF; used to promote the growth of white blood cells), blood clotting factor 7 (for the treatment of hemophilia), erythropoietin (a drug used to treat kidney failure), streptokinase (a drug administered in heart attacks), and human growth hormone. Some of these products have been spectacular commercial successes. Global sales of erythropoietin drugs in 2006, for example, were about $13.9 billion. Worldwide sales of recombinant DNA drugs amounted to more than $32 billion in the same year. At the time, sales had been increasing at a rate of about 28 percent a year over the preceding decade.

The first drug to be produced using recombinant DNA methods was insulin. In 1979, researchers at Eli Lilly and Company devised a procedure for synthesizing insulin using the common bacterium *E. coli*. The procedure was approved by the U.S. Food and Drug Administration in 1982, and genetically modified human insulin became commercially available in that year under the trade name of Humulin®.

Insulin consists of two chains, designated as the A-chain and the B-chain, as shown in the diagram on page 67. The two chains are joined by two disulfide (-S-S-) bonds. The A-chain contains 21 amino acid residues, and the B-chain has 30 amino acid residues.

Human insulin differs slightly from cow, pig, sheep, horse, and other forms of insulin, as shown in the table on page 68. For the vast majority of diabetics, these differences are irrelevant. Bovine (cow), porcine (pig), and some other forms of animal insulin can be pharmaceutically used as substitutes for human insulin. About 5 percent of all diabetics experience reactions to animal insulin, however, and for such individuals, only insulin taken from human sources can be used as a replacement drug in the treatment of their diabetes.

In the Lilly recombinant DNA approach, the genes (oligonucleotides) coding for the A-chain and the B-chain were synthesized chemically and then attached to the *E. coli* gene coding for the enzyme β-galactosidase. When the genetically modified genes began to express themselves, they produced molecules of β-galactosidase to which were attached either the A-chain or the B-chain of the insulin molecule.

At this point, the bond joining the β-galactosidase fragment to the insulin chains was broken with cyanogen bromide (CNBr). The free insulin chains were then removed, purified, and treated with a sulfating agent to generate disulfide bonds, joining the two chains to each other and producing an exact copy of human insulin.

The development of a recombinant DNA method for producing insulin synthetically was a remarkable achievement. However, it

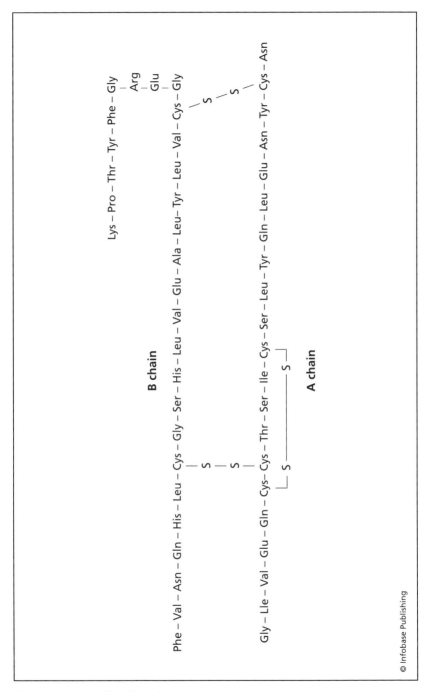

Primary structure of insulin molecule

turned out to be only the first step in the design and synthesis of a group of compounds chemically and biologically related to natural insulin. These compounds are, as a group, known as *insulin analogs.* Insulin analogs have been developed to meet a number of specialized requirements that will improve the health outlook of diabetics.

The first such analog to have been developed was lispro (Humalog®), first approved for use in the United States in June 1996. In lispro, the sequence of the next-to-last and third-to-last amino acids in the B-chain (positions 28 and 29; proline and lysine) are reversed. As a result of this change, patients absorb an

◁ VARIATIONS IN INSULINS FROM VARIOUS SOURCES* ▷

SPECIES	AMINO ACID POSITION						
	A8	A9	A10	B1	B2	B27	B30
Human	Thr	Ser	Ile	Phe	Val	Thr	Thr
Cow	Ala	Ser	Val	Phe	Val	Thr	Ala
Sheep	Ala	Gly	Val	Phe	Val	Thr	Ala
Horse	Thr	Gly	Ile	Phe	Val	Thr	Ala
Pig	Thr	Ser	Ile	Phe	Val	Thr	Ala
Rabbit	Thr	Ser	Ile	Phe	Val	Thr	Ser
Dog	Thr	Ser	Ile	Phe	Val	Thr	Ala
Chicken	His	Asn	Thr	Ala	Ala	Ser	Ala
Duck	Glu	Asn	Pro	Ala	Ala	Ser	Thr

*All residues other than those shown are identical.

insulin molecule more rapidly, and it reaches higher serum levels in a shorter time than is the case with natural insulin. Most important, lispro behaves in the same way physiologically as does natural insulin.

Another genetically modified fast-acting insulin is called aspart (NovoLog®). In this analog, the proline residue in position 28 of the B-chain is replaced with aspartic acid. The biological effects of this change are similar to those with lispro: The modified insulin is absorbed more rapidly and reaches a higher serum level than is the case with natural insulin. Again, it functions in essentially the same way as natural insulin in reducing blood sugar levels.

Insulin analogs with other specialized properties have also been developed. In some cases, the goal of researchers was to modify the natural insulin molecule so as to prolong the drug's action. One product designed for this purpose is NovoSol Basal. In this analog, the threonine residue in position 27 of the B-chain is replaced by arginine, the asparagine residue in position 21 of the A-chain is replaced by glycine, and the alanine residue in position 30 of the B-chain is replaced by threonine. NovoSol Basal turned out to meet the requirement of remaining in the bloodstream longer than natural insulin, but it was less efficient in metabolizing blood glucose and the research program designed for its development was canceled.

An apparently more effective method for prolonging the half-life of insulin in the blood is to add substituents at the end of the A- or B-chain (or both) that alter the chemical properties of the molecule and delay its breakdown in the body. A product known as HOE 901 (insulin glargine) has two glycine residues added to one end of the B-chain and the A21 asparagine residue replaced with another glycine residue. These changes modify the acidity of the insulin molecule, reducing the rate at which it is absorbed and metabolized in the body.

Another approach to the development of long-lasting insulin is illustrated in an experimental product known as insulin detemir. This insulin analog is produced by adding a fatty acid to the end of the B-chain, increasing its ability to bond to albumin in the blood. After this bonding occurs, the insulin is released at a slow and constant rate over a period of at least 24 hours.

These examples illustrate the flexibility of drug design possible with the use of recombinant DNA techniques. In many other instances, analogs of some basic compound have been developed with a range of physical, chemical, biological, and pharmacological properties that permit their use in a variety of medical situations.

The second drug synthesized by recombinant DNA methods was human growth hormone. Human growth hormone is the most abundant hormone produced by the pituitary gland. It is far larger and more complex than human insulin, consisting of 191 amino acids. The hormone is also known by a number of other names, including somatotropin, pituitary growth hormone, adenohypophyseal growth hormone, and anterior pituitary growth hormone. It is often abbreviated as HGH, hGH, rGH, or rHGH. The recombinant forms of the drug are sold under various product names, including Genotropin® (Pfizer, Inc.), Humatrope® (Eli Lilly and Company), Norditropin® (NovoNordisk), Nutropin® and Protropin® (Genentech), and Saizen® and Serostim® (Serono®). The recombinant form of HGH was approved for use in the United States in 1985 for the treatment of growth deficiencies in children.

A number of forms of human growth hormone are produced by recombinant DNA technology. All are structurally similar (but not identical) to each other. The earliest form was nearly identical to the naturally occurring form of the hormone, the difference being a single methionine residue added at one end of the molecule. That form of the product was originally marketed under the trade name of Protropin®. Somewhat later, another form of the hormone was manufactured that is identical to natural HGH; that is, it lacks the methionine residue found in Protropin®. The product known as Saizen® is an example of this form of the product. Other forms of the hormone currently available in the United States are Nutropin®, Humatrope®, Genotropin®, Norditropin®, and Tev-Tropin®.

The U.S. Food and Drug Administration has now approved about 50 drugs prepared by recombinant DNA techniques for use in humans. An additional 200 products are at various stages of development and testing. Some of the approved products and the uses for which they are permitted are listed in the chart on page 71.

◄ SOME APPROVED RECOMBINANT DNA DRUGS ►

DRUG	YEAR APPROVED	APPROVED USE
Human insulin	1982	Diabetes mellitus
Human growth hormone	1985	Growth deficiency in children
Interferon-alpha-2b	1986 and later	Hairy cell leukemia, genital warts, Kaposi's sarcoma, hepatitis B, hepatitis C
Interferon-alpha-2a	1986 and later	Hairy cell leukemia, Kaposi's sarcoma
Hepatitis B vaccine	1986 and later	Hepatitis B
Alterplase	1987 and later	Acute myocardial infarction and acute massive pulmonary embolism
Antihemophiliac factor	1992	Hemophilia A
Interferon-beta-1b	1993	Certain types of multiple sclerosis
Imiglucerase (for injection)	1994	Gaucher's disease
Coagulation factor IX	1997	Factor IX deficiencies (e.g., Christmas disease)

Recombinant DNA technology has shown itself to be one of the most powerful techniques for the development of new drugs. It has resulted in the creation of a host of new products used to treat a range of diseases safely and at relatively low cost.

Pharming as a Source of Genetically Modified Drugs

Recombinant DNA drug production has been a success story, but the technology does have its drawbacks and disadvantages. For example, the use of bacterial plasmids and, less commonly, viruses, as vectors for the insertion of genes into host cells has its limitations. While such methods work well for smaller drug molecules, such as insulin, they are much less effective in the production of larger, more complex proteins that constitute many of the drugs that chemists would like to manufacture synthetically.

In addition, commercial facilities for the production of recombinant DNA drugs such as insulin using bacterial plasmids are generally much more complex than might be imagined from the description in the previous section. The broth in which engineered bacteria are kept must be maintained at constant temperature, nutrients must be added regularly, and the whole system must be kept free of pathogens. Systems such as these can be, in short, quite expensive.

For more than a decade, researchers have been exploring an alternative to recombinant DNA methods using bacterial plasmids for the production of drugs. The new methods make use of farm animals (and, more recently, plants) as hosts for the transplantation of genes that code for the production of certain desired proteins that can be used as drugs. This new field of research has been given the name *pharming* to indicate its hybrid character, which combines the knowledge and methods of *phar*macy with those of far*ming*.

In some ways, the use of animals (almost always mammals) as substitutes for bacteria in the recombinant DNA production of drugs is a natural and obvious extension of the techniques originally developed for the manufacture of insulin, human growth hormone, and other pharmaceuticals. Live animals have a built-in production system in which temperature, pH (a measure of the acidity of a solution), and a natural immune system provide an ideal environment for the culturing and harvesting of drugs produced from transplanted genes. They also provide themselves with all the nutrients needed to keep the "system" operating and possess a natural "output" system in the form of urine, blood, and/or milk from which the manufactured drugs can be collected.

One of the earliest experiments in the field of pharming was conducted by researchers from PPL Therapeutics, the organization that owns the technology used in the cloning of the first mammal, the sheep Dolly. PPL researchers transplanted the gene for the production of a protein known as alpha-1-antitrypsin (AAT) into the DNA of a sheep named Tracy. AAT is a protein normally produced in the liver and transported to the lungs, where it is used to support normal breathing. People lacking in protein are short of breath and have trouble breathing when carrying out even simple activities.

The scientists at PPL attached the gene that codes for AAT to a gene in Tracy's DNA that codes for the production of milk. When the sheep gave milk, the milk contained small amounts of alpha-1-antitrypsin. All researchers had to do was collect Tracy's milk and separate the AAT from it. Since the AAT gene had been inserted into the sheep's DNA, it was passed on to her progeny and to succeeding generations of descendants, which, therefore, had the same capacity to produce alpha-1-antitrypsin-laced milk. By 1998, PPL researchers estimated that Tracy had more than 800 granddaughters, which were producing about 15 grams of AAT per liter of milk. At that point, the company began clinical trials for the use of the engineered protein for the treatment of people with cystic fibrosis in the United Kingdom.

About four years into the trial, some troubling results began to appear. Patients using the engineered AAT developed "wheezing" symptoms, for which no explanation could be found. The company decided to delay further testing of the drug in human patients until they could better understand this unexpected problem. They continued to be optimistic about commercial use of the drug, however, and predicted that it would become available to the general public in 2007.

Pharming and Transgenic Technology

Animals like Tracy are known as *transgenic* animals because they contain genes from two different animals. Tracy was transgenic because she carried human DNA inserted into her own sheep DNA.

The first step in producing a transgenic animal is to inject the desired gene (such as the gene for AAT) into a fertilized cell of the host animal using a micropipette (a tube used to deliver small quantities of liquids). In some fraction of cases, the gene is then incorporated into the host's DNA. Laboratory workers analyze the fertilized cells to see which have incorporated the guest gene into their own DNA. These transgenic cells are then inserted into the surrogate mother's uterus (such as the uterus of a sheep) and allowed to develop. When the cell becomes an embryo and is eventually born as a new animal, it is "normal" in all respects except that it carries an additional gene for the production of the desired protein. Furthermore, the inserted gene has become part of the animal's genome (its DNA), so that it is transmitted to future generations.

Completing this sequence of events successfully is very difficult. Many problems can occur at any stage of the process, preventing the successful incorporation of the guest gene into the host DNA or preventing the transmission of the modified DNA to future generations. In one experiment, 152 female sheep were implanted with the gene for AAT, of which 112 gave birth to live lambs. Of these lambs, only one male and four females carried the AAT gene, and, of this number, only a single female gave birth to a transgenic offspring.

Given these odds, one wonders about the economic viability of this technique: The cost of producing a single transgenic animal ranges from a few tens of thousands to a few hundreds of thousands of dollars. The only additional factor that *does* make the process economically viable is the return. Companies involved in the development of transgenic animals for drug production estimate that a single transgenic animal may be able to produce up the $300 million worth of pharmaceuticals during its lifetime.

As of late 2006, no pharm-produced drug had as yet been approved for human use by the U.S. Food and Drug Administration. A number of products were "in the pipeline," however, at various stages of the testing and development process that are required for FDA approval. The following chart lists only a few of the many drugs obtained from pharming practices now being tested.

◁ SOME PHARM-DRUGS CURRENTLY IN DEVELOPMENT ▷

DRUG	HOST ANIMAL	INTENDED TREATMENT
Alpha-1-antitrypsin	Sheep	Emphysema, cystic fibrosis, other lung disorders
Tissue plasminogen activator	Sheep, pig	Thrombosis (dissolves blood clots)
Factor VIII and factor IX	Sheep, pig, cow	Hemophilia
Fibrinogen	Sheep, cow	Healing of wounds
Human protein C	Goat	Thrombosis
Glutamic acid decarboxylase	Goat	Type 1 diabetes mellitus
Alpha-lactalbumin	Cow	Anti-infective
Collagen I and II	Cow	Anti-arthritic; tissue repair
Lactoferrin	Cow	Anti-arthritic; gastrointestinal tract infections
Erythropoietin	Rabbit	Anemia resulting from dialysis
Human growth hormone	Rat	Pituitary dwarfism

The most recent twist in the use of recombinant DNA technology to produce drugs has been the development of transgenic plants with many of the capabilities of transgenic animals. Some authorities refer to this field of research as *molecular farming* and call the products of their research *farmaceuticals.*

One of the most active companies involved in this field of research is the San Diego Company Epicyte Biopharmaceutical. Epicyte has developed a system for introducing genes coding for desired proteins into the DNA of various plants—most commonly, corn. The company calls its system Plantibodies™ technology. One of its first endeavors was the insertion of genes for the production of secretory antibodies into corn plants. Secretory antibodies are natural proteins produced by the human body that coat the wet, warm epithelial tissue found in body linings, such as those found in the gut and inside the mouth. When these genes are expressed in a corn plant, secretory antibodies are produced within corn kernels. When the corn is harvested, the antibodies can be extracted from the corn kernels, purified, and prepared for human use.

One possible application for antibodies prepared by this method is as contraceptives (fertility preventatives). Since they coat the epithelial tissue lining of a woman's vagina, secretory antibodies provide natural protection against invading bodies, such as sperm, killing them and preventing fertilization of an ovum. A second use is as protection against certain viral diseases such as hepatitis. Again, antibodies recognize, attack, and kill viruses responsible for the disease. In 2003, the company also announced the development of antibodies against human HIV produced from corn plants. The antibodies work by binding proteins needed for the synthesis of the HIV virus.

An area of research that seems to be especially fruitful is the development of engineered plants with genes coding for disease preventatives—that is, vaccines. A person could receive a vaccine and thus be protected against diseases in an entirely new way: by eating a therapeutic food. Currently, researchers are exploring the possibility of inserting genes for vaccines against measles, polio, diphtheria, yellow fever, various forms of viral diarrhea, and other diseases.

An example of this line of research is an engineered tomato plant developed by researchers at the Arizona Biomedical Institute. The tomato plant carried the gene that codes for the production of a vaccine against hepatitis B. Scientists obtained enough of the anti-hepatitis vaccine for 4,000 doses from just 30 tomato plants. The tomato juice from which the vaccine is obtained can be freeze-dried and stored almost indefinitely.

The chart on page 78 lists some examples of the diseases for which pharmed drugs are currently being sought and some of the plant hosts in which those experiments are being carried out.

Today, there are more than 400 plant-based drugs under development in the United States alone. None has yet completed the necessary trials and been approved by the FDA, although some industry observers expect the first such approval to be awarded within a few years.

Pros and Cons of Pharming

The use of recombinant DNA technology to produce drugs from engineered plants and animals holds enormous promise and some substantial risks. Probably the most important benefit to be derived from pharming is cheaper production. As noted earlier in this chapter, the cost of developing a single transgenic animal or strain of engineered plant can be substantial, in the tens or hundreds of thousands of dollars, but once that animal or plant has been bred, the financial returns are substantial. According to one study, the cost of a drug produced by pharming techniques may be as low as $10 to $100 per gram, compared with current costs of more than $1,000 per gram by conventional techniques.

Pharming also promises to provide faster and more flexible processes for the manufacture of pharmaceuticals. Corporations can adapt well-established, easily accessible host organisms (such as cows, pigs, sheep, maize, tobacco, and soybeans) to a new function—the production of drugs—at relatively modest cost. For example, one drug company has said that the leaves from only 26 tobacco plants could produce enough of the engineered enzyme glucocerebrosidase,

◁ **SOME DISEASES FOR WHICH DRUGS
ARE CURRENTLY BEING DEVELOPED
BY PHARMING TECHNOLOGIES** ▷

DISEASE	PLANT
Dental caries	Tobacco
Cancer (various forms)	Wheat, rice, tobacco
B-cell lymphoma	Tobacco
Herpes simplex	Soybean, tobacco, potato, lupin, lettuce
Rabies	Tomato
Human cytomegalovirus	Tobacco
Hypopituitary dwarfism	Tobacco
Human lactoferrin deficiency*	Rice
Human lysozyme deficiency*	Rice
Enterotoxigenic *E. Coli*	Tobacco, tomato, maize
Cholera	Potato
Norwalk virus	Tobacco, potato
Rabbit hemorrhagic disease virus	Potato
Foot-and-mouth disease (agricultural domestic animals)	*Arabidopsis thaliana* (mustard family), alfalfa
Transmissible gastroenteritis coronavirus (pigs)	*Arabidopsis thaliana* (mustard family), alfalfa, maize

*vulnerability to infection

one of the most expensive drugs now available, to treat a patient with Gaucher's disease for a year.

Savings in production would almost certainly be translated into savings for consumers. For example, pharming technology developed for the production of the enzyme alpha-galactosidase, used in the treatment of Fabry's disease, could be reduced by 90 percent, dropping the cost of treating a single patient from its current level of about $400,000 per year to about $40,000 per year.

Consumers would also benefit from having access to drugs that currently cannot be produced by conventional manufacturing processes, or only at great expense. One example that has commonly been mentioned is a new monoclonal antibody that has been shown to be effective in the prevention of tooth decay. The cost of producing this drug by traditional means is prohibitive. Its projected cost by the use of engineered tobacco plants, however, places it well within the range of what consumers will be able to afford.

Edible vaccines are another new and attractive product of pharming technology. At the present time, vaccines are almost always administered by injection. The sight of a medical worker's needle has long been a source of anguish for individuals of all ages, but especially young children. The recombinant methods just described, if successful, would allow necessary vaccines to be introduced into transgenic organisms and then eaten by those who need to be vaccinated, essentially causing no discomfort or emotional stress. Reducing the cost of drugs and providing them in more palatable forms is also likely to extend the availability of pharmaceuticals to parts of the world—primarily, developing nations—where such medical care is now completely absent or, at least, less readily available than it is in developed nations.

Like any other new technology, pharming not only holds some glowing promises, as outlined above, but also poses some significant risks, both to people and to the environment. One of the most dramatic of these risks is the harm that such drugs may cause to patients who use them.

Researchers have anticipated that engineered drugs would pose essentially no harm to humans since they are chemically identical to proteins produced naturally in the human body. As it turns out, however, this is not necessarily the case. For example, in mid-2002, a number of reports surfaced about the risks posed by the genetically engineered drug Eprex®, developed and manufactured by the drug firm Johnson & Johnson. The drug is a recombinant formulation of erythropoietin, a protein that induces the production of red blood cells. It is used for individuals who have anemia, an inadequate supply of red blood cells in their bodies. In at least 140 cases, patients' immune systems have rejected the Eprex® protein, treating it as an infectious invader that must be destroyed. Even worse, immune systems then go on to attack the few red blood cells that patients' bodies are making naturally, resulting in an even more severe case of anemia (known as pure red cell aplasia) than had existed before use of the drug.

Johnson & Johnson researchers say that they currently have no explanation for this unexpected response to Eprex®. Interestingly enough, no similar immune response has been observed with either another of Johnson & Johnson's recombinant erythropoietins, Procrit®, or with a competitor's comparable product, Amgen's Epogen®.

Part of the problem in dealing with transgenically produced drugs such as Eprex® is that engineered drugs tend to fall into a gray area of regulatory responsibility: They are not exactly foods, nor are they traditional drugs. So regulatory agencies, such as the Food and Drug Administration in the United States, have not yet developed regulatory guidelines for their manufacture, testing, and distribution.

That deficiency troubles critics of pharming, who see a number of ways in which engineered products could escape into the environment, become part of the human or animal food chain, and possibly affect the environment itself. For instance, in late 2000 food companies were forced to issue a massive recall of certain corn products, including corn chips and tortillas, because they contained small amounts of an engineered product called StarLink™ that had not been approved for human consumption. StarLink™ DNA contains a gene for the production of a pesticide that is supposed to protect the corn while it is growing, as a substitute for the addition of chemical pesticides on the land on which the corn is planted. That pesticide, however, was found to have induced allergic reactions in humans who ate the engineered corn.

Unfortunately, there is more than one way that engineered genes might escape from the plants into which they were inserted and affect humans directly or become part of the "natural" plant environment. Some of these mechanisms are as follows:

➤ Accidental grazing of farm animals in areas where modified plants are growing;

➤ Inadequate disposal of wastes from engineered plants;

➤ Accidental mixing of engineered plant material with food intended for human consumption or as feed for domestic animals;

➤ Accidental inhalation, consumption, or topical contact by workers with engineered plant products;

➤ Cross-pollination between engineered and nonengineered plants in the field;

➤ Transmission of engineered plant pollen or other plant parts by grazing wildlife, bees and other pollinating insects, and organisms that live in the soil;

➤ Possible accumulation of engineered genes in the food chain; and

➤ Possible persistence of engineered plant products in the soil.

Biotechnology and pharmaceutical companies are well aware of such concerns and are attempting to develop environments in which engineered plants and animals are isolated from the surrounding environment and in which manufactured drugs are extracted, isolated, and purified under safe conditions. A vitally important factor in the eventual success or failure of the use of engineered drugs is, of course, public confidence in their safety and efficacy. It only makes sense, then, for companies to employ safe techniques at every step of the process by which such drugs are produced.

Another question remains, however: How much risk in the production of pharmed drugs is the general public willing to accept in exchange for the benefits they may be able to provide, not only for

Americans but also for people in developed and developing nations around the world? It seems clear that there is probably no way of mass-producing engineered drugs without some risk to humans, domestic animals, and the biological environment. On the other hand, the availability of those drugs may save untold numbers of human and animal lives and immeasurably improve the health of people and animals around the world.

4

DESIGNER DRUGS

Charlene was really excited. This was the first rave party to which she had ever been invited. She tried to act as if she were an old hand at raves. After all, most of her friends were quite a bit older than she was, and she did not want them to snicker at their 15-year-old friend who had never even heard about raves until a few months ago. Probably the best thing about the party, Charlene thought, was all the new people she would meet. Her friends had promised to introduce her to all their "good friends" at the rave: Adam and Eve, Stacy, and Tango and Cash. Now that she was here, she felt a bit foolish to find out those "friends" were actually drugs, "club drugs" as her friends called them. She was not sure she wanted to try the drugs, but then what would her friends have said? "Just a kid," probably, or "What a chicken!" So, how much could it hurt if she took just a couple of pills? She knew enough to be careful when taking drugs she did not know anything about.

Now she really was not feeling very well. Her skin felt all clammy, she was nauseous, and she felt as if she could hardly breathe. Maybe she should say something to Eric or Ben or Juanita or Holly. Or maybe she should just wait a while and see if she felt better, but everything was getting so blurry.

Charlene was getting her first introduction to *designer drugs.* Designer drugs are also known by other names, such as *"club drugs"* or *"rave drugs."* Adam, Eve, Stacy, and Tango and Cash are *street names,* slang names or nicknames by which some designer drugs

83

are known. The use of recreational designer drugs has become a troubling phenomenon in the United States and other parts of the world. Such drugs may cause serious physical and health problems for people who use them, and they are often implicated in a variety of crimes committed by people looking for ways to finance their drug habits.

Concerns about drug use are not new in the United States. As far back as the early 20th century, many people argued against the dangers of alcohol abuse. (The term *alcohol* in general use refers to ethanol, or ethyl alcohol, C_2H_5OH.) Feelings were strong enough that the nation eventually adopted the Eighteenth Amendment to the U.S. Constitution in 1920. That amendment prohibited the manufacture, sale, or transportation of intoxicating liquors within the United States. That amendment was later nullified by the adoption of the Twenty-first Amendment to the constitution in 1933.

Public attention next turned to the dangers posed by marijuana, culminating in a now-famous motion picture released in 1936 entitled *Reefer Madness.* That film tells the story of a group of teenagers who are lured into marijuana use, leading to a sequence of tragedies that includes a hit-and-run accident, manslaughter, suicide, rape, and, ultimately, descent into madness for all. Fears about the dangers of marijuana and drugs such as heroin and cocaine have continued, albeit in not quite as dramatic a fashion as portrayed in *Reefer Madness,* to the present day. The lead federal agency in the fight against illegal drug use since 1973 has been the Drug Enforcement Agency (DEA), a division of the Department of Justice. Today the DEA has a staff of nearly 11,000 employees and an annual budget of about $2.4 billion.

During the 1990s, a new source of concern about drug use arose focusing on designer drugs. Some observers warned of an epidemic of illegal drug use in the late 1990s, centering on newly synthesized products such as methamphetamine, gamma-hydroxybutyrate, fentanyl, and rohypnol and their analogs. Between 1990 and 2000, for example, the number of first-time users of one designer drug, popularly known as Ecstasy, rose from about 200,000 to nearly 2 million individuals. During the same period, the number of Ecstasy-related deaths soared from zero to 76.

What Are Designer Drugs?

The term *designer drugs* has at least two meanings. First, it is used to describe new kinds of medications being developed for the treatment of a variety of diseases and disorders. The field of study out of which such drugs develop is called *pharmacogenomics,* a combination of two terms referring to the study of drugs (*pharmacy*) and the study of genetics (*genomics*). Second, the term *designer drugs* is used to refer to a number of synthetic chemicals that are derivatives of legal drugs developed for use in recreational settings, such as the "rave" described above.

Amazing progress has been made over the past century in developing a host of synthetic chemicals that can be used for the treatment of disease. In one respect, however, that progress has been based on a somewhat crude model of drug development and use. In the vast majority of cases, any given drug is known to have some *general* effect on a particular disease for *most* individuals. For example, physicians tend to prescribe aspirin for patients who have moderate levels of pain, fever, or other medical problems. Physicians also know that aspirin can have varying levels of success in treating pain, fever, and other conditions, such that low dosages are very effective in some individuals and not at all effective in others. Also, some patients may experience undesirable or dangerous side effects when they use aspirin.

This is true of nearly all drugs available to the medical profession today. In many cases, a doctor may have to experiment with a variety of medications

Ecstasy, shown here in pill form, produces feelings of elation and well-being but also causes dangerous side effects that include dehydration, loss of control and appetite, and memory and weight loss. (SPL/Photo Researchers, Inc.)

(aspirin versus ibuprofen versus acetaminophen, for example) at various dosages before finding exactly the right treatment for any one individual. "Getting it right" in prescribing a drug, then, is often a matter of trial and error that wastes time and money and may have harmful effects on a patient.

Researchers are now learning a great deal more about the specific details of particular diseases as well as the way that individual patients respond to drug therapy. Cancer therapy that makes use of synthetic chemicals (chemotherapy) is an example. In the past, researchers have somewhat randomly experimented with a variety of toxic chemicals found to be effective in killing cancer cells in experimental animals and, eventually, in humans. The approach has usually been to give the toxic chemical to an animal or person with cancer in the hope that the chemical will kill enough cancer cells to cure the disease or arrest its development. Of course, the toxic chemical also kills many healthy cells, resulting in unpleasant and often dangerous side effects for the patient.

One new approach to drug development involves acquiring a vastly improved understanding of how a disease such as cancer originally develops. Research may show that cells begin to produce abnormal forms of an essential biochemical, that cells cease producing the biochemical entirely, or that they alter the production of the biochemical in some other way so as to result in the development of a tumor. Learning more about that process generally means finding the specific aberrant molecule responsible for development of the tumor and finding a way to destroy or block the formation of that molecule.

The development of a drug known as imatinib (Glivec®, Gleevic®, or ST1571), is an example of this process. Imatinib has been found to be effective in the treatment of Philadelphia chromosome–positive chronic myeloid leukemia (Ph+CML), a condition that affects about 7,000 new patients in the United States each year. Researchers discovered that Ph+CML occurs when changes in a person's DNA result in the formation of an abnormal gene that codes for the uninterrupted production of white blood cells. They determined that one possible method for treating this condition was to synthesize a drug that blocks the enzyme by binding to its active site and preventing its further operation.

This approach was very different from the traditional method for making anticancer drugs, that is, finding a toxic chemical that could be sent into the body to kill cancer cells (and healthy cells associated with them). Instead, chemists discovered the molecular structure of the aberrant molecule (the Ph+CML enzyme) and designed a new chemical (imatinib) to react precisely and uniquely with that molecule. When a patient is treated with that chemical, it goes specifically to the single molecule responsible for the patient's medical disorder, inactivating the molecule and ameliorating the disease. The chemical has a very high probability of success in treating one very specific type of disorder, but it has a very low probability of being effective against other types of cancer caused by other biochemical mechanisms. That means that the anticancer "toolkit" available to physicians in the future may consist not of a relatively small number of highly toxic chemicals that kill a great variety of healthy and abnormal cells but rather a very large number of specially designed chemicals—*designer drugs*—each with its very specific task to perform in fighting disease.

Designer drugs of this kind might be called *disease-directed designer drugs,* or DDDD, because they are invented to attack highly specific medical conditions. A second type of designer drug might be called *patient-directed designer drugs,* or PDDD. Such drugs have become possible largely as a result of new information obtained as the result of the Human Genome Project and similar research on human molecular genetics. These studies have provided scientists with a vastly improved understanding of the nature of human DNA, the way DNA differs from individual to individual, and the role of specific DNA sequences in the development of medical disorders. Scientists now know the structure and function of each nucleotide sequence (gene) in the human genome and, in many cases, understand how variations in nucleotide sequences result in the development of a medical disorder.

One of the important discoveries resulting from human genome research is an understanding of the extent to which genetic structure varies from person to person, between genders, among ethnic and racial groups, and throughout other groups of humans. One obvious example is the much greater number of estrogen receptors present in women's bodies compared with the number in men's bodies. Genomic research was not needed to determine this variation, but it does provide a reminder of how different the genetic structure of individuals and groups can be.

A dramatic example of the kind of genetic information that has become available to medical researchers is a study conducted in 2003 by researchers at McGill University in Montreal directed by Jeffrey Mogil. Mogil's team made that rather remarkable discovery that fair-skinned redheaded women respond better to a pain medication called pentazocine than do non-fair-skinned redheaded women or men of any description. They found that the reason for this phenomenon is that a particular gene called the melanocortin-1 receptor gene (Mc1r) appears to have a role in determining both hair and skin color and the ways in which a person responds to a particular chemical (pentazocine, in this case). The obvious conclusion from the study is that a drug that might be effective for some individuals because of their particular genetic makeup might have no value for other individuals with differing genetic characteristics.

One great contribution that genetic information can make to drug design is to reduce adverse drug reactions. Adverse drug reactions (ADRs) are instances in which a person has negative, generally unexpected, effects after taking some prescribed medication. In the United States, about 2.1 million ADRs are reported each year, about half of which require hospitalization and 100,000 of which result in death. ADRs are the fifth leading cause of death in the United States.

At least one factor leading to ADRs is the mismatch between a prescribed medication and the specific genetic make up of the patient who takes the drug. The patient may lack the gene that properly metabolizes the drug or may metabolize it incorrectly, converting it into a toxic chemical. If medical workers have access to a patient's genetic composition, however, they will be able to prescribe drugs that more closely match not only his or her medical needs but also his or her body's ability to utilize them properly.

Illegal Designer Drugs

Notwithstanding the remarkable advances being made in therapeutic drug production, most people who hear the term *designer drugs* today probably do not think of the new kinds of medications described in the preceding section. Instead, they are more likely to associate the term with a group of illegal drugs produced for recreational purposes, generally by amateur chemists working out of clandestine laboratories. Although there is no universally accepted meaning for the term *designer drugs,* one researcher in the field, J. F. Buchanan, has provided one definition:

"'Designer drugs' are substances intended for recreational use which are derivatives of approved drugs [developed] so as to circumvent existing legal restrictions."

The term *designer drug* was probably first used in 1968 by Gary Henderson, a chemist at the University of California at Davis. Henderson defined designer drugs as "substances where the psychoactive properties of a drug are retained, but the molecular structure has been altered to avoid prosecution."

The use of certain types of drugs for recreational purposes is probably as old as humankind. In virtually all human cultures that have been studied, at least some individuals use some types of recreational drugs at least some of the time in order to reach transcendental ("out-of-body") experiences. In many cases, those experiences are imbued with mystical or religious significance. For example, the use of peyote, a member of the cactus family, has been a part of the culture of Native American tribes for thousands of years. The active ingredient in peyote is mescaline, a hallucinogenic compound, that is, a substance that triggers in the user the perception of sights, sounds, or other sensual experiences that do not actually exist or that are not apparent to other people. Even today, many Native American tribes use peyote in ages-old ceremonies that constitute sacramental experiences in their religions.

Historically, the vast majority of drugs used for recreational purposes have been plant products: alcohol (from fermented grains and

◄ U.S. DRUG ENFORCEMENT ADMINISTRATION ►

"**W**e're always trying to stay one step ahead of our competitors!" That slogan could be used by both sides in the battle between the producers and sellers of illegal designer drugs and governmental agencies whose responsibility it is to protect the U.S. public against such drugs. One of the three most important federal agencies involved in that ongoing struggle is the U.S. Drug Enforcement Administration (DEA).

The DEA was established under Executive Order 11727, issued by President Richard M. Nixon on July 10, 1973. This action was part of the more general Reorganization Plan 2 intended to streamline the operation of the federal government. Nixon saw the DEA as constituting a major force in the "all-out global war on the drug menace" that he wanted to promote. The agency's first administrator was John R. Bartels, Jr., a former federal prosecutor and previously deputy director of the Office of Drug Abuse Law Enforcement (ODALE), which Nixon had established within the Department of Justice only a year earlier.

The federal government's efforts to control the production, distribution, and use of illegal drugs date back to 1915, when the Bureau of Internal

fruits), peyote (from a member of the cactus family, *Lophophora williamsii*), tobacco (from the plant *Nicotiana tabacum*), hemp (*Cannabis sativa*), opium (*Papaver somniferum*), and "magic" mushrooms (from a number of genera, most commonly that of the *Psilocybe* genus). In recent decades, however, another source of recreational drugs has become available: existing chemical products, often with well-known, carefully studied, and widely used properties, that have been chemically modified. This source of recreational drugs has become available because of a simple but far-reaching discovery made by chemists decades ago, namely that alterations in the chemical structure of a molecule can be made that result in the production of a new product that may have chemical, physiological, and pharmacological properties similar to those of the original molecule. The modifications produced in this way are generally known as *chemical analogs.*

An example of this phenomenon is the group of drugs known as the *sulfa* drugs. The parent compound of that family is sulfanilamide,

Revenue was established within the Department of the Treasury (DOT) and assigned these responsibilities. Over the years, drug enforcement responsibilities were transferred to the Bureau of Prohibition of the DOT (1927–30) and later to the Bureau of Narcotics of the DOT (1930–68) and the Bureau of Drug Abuse Control of the Food and Drug Administration (1966–68). Drug enforcement authority was consolidated in one agency again in 1968 in the Department of Justice's Bureau of Narcotics and Dangerous Drugs (1968–73) before the establishment of the DEA. Since 1973, the DEA has been one of three agencies responsible for drug control activities in the United States. The other two agencies are the White House Office of National Drug Control Policy (ONDCP), established by the Anti-Drug Abuse Act of 1988, and the Food and Drug Administration (FDA).

One of the DEA's most important functions is enforcement of the Controlled Substances Act of 1970 (see table on pages 5–6), which provides the basis for classifying chemical compounds into one of five "schedules," based on their potential for medical use and misuse by the general public. In addition to investigating, apprehending, and prosecuting individuals and groups in violation of this act, the DEA works with local, state, and international agencies to reduce the availability of illicit drugs in the marketplace.

discovered by the German biochemist Gerhard Domagk (1895–1964) in 1936. Sulfanilamide was one of the first synthetic antibiotics to have been discovered. It was widely used during World War II and is credited with having saved untold numbers of lives because of its antibacterial action. As effective as it was, however, it did have some undesirable side effects, and chemists searched for ways of modifying the sulfanilamide molecule so as to retain the compound's therapeutic effects, while reducing its unwanted side effects. Over time, they invented a number of chemical analogs of sulfanilamide—including sulfacetamide, sulfamethoxazole, sulfasalazine, and sulfisoxazole— each effective in its own way and each a satisfactory alternative for the original compound in certain applications.

The motivation for the production of designer drugs has always been quite different from that described for the production of sulfanilamide analogs, however. Chemists who synthesize designer drugs do so primarily for the purpose of avoiding legal restrictions

This Persian miniature dating to the 15th century is a reminder that people have been using drugs for recreational purposes for centuries. The noblewoman shown here is probably smoking hashish through a hookah pipe. (National Library of Medicine)

on the production and sale of compounds that have been declared illegal by the government. Such compounds have generally been classified by the U.S. government as Schedule I or Schedule II drugs—that is, drugs that have high potential for abuse, that have some or no currently accepted medical use in treatment in the United States, that lack any accepted safety for use under medical supervision, and/or that have a potential for abuse that may lead to severe psychological or physical dependence. The manufacture, sale, and use of such drugs is prohibited and can result in serious fines. The market for such drugs among the general public is, however, very large, and the profits to be made from meeting this demand are comparably great. It is possible, for example, to make drugs worth in excess of a million dollars for no more than a few hundred dollars in raw materials. For this reason, the substances generally known as *designer drugs* are often known also among experts in the field as *controlled substance analogs,* or CSAs.

Fentanyl Analogs

One of the earliest forays into the development of designer drugs was the mid-1970s production of analogs of the legal drug fentanyl. Fentanyl was first synthesized in 1960 at the Belgian pharmaceutical firm of Janssen Pharmaceutica and first made commercially available five years later under the trade name of Fentanyl® or Sublimaze®. The drug was designed for use as an intravenous anesthetic. It is about 100 times as potent as morphine but acts over a very short period, usually no more than about 30 minutes. It is currently the world's most widely used anesthetic and is used in about 70 percent of all surgeries in the United States. A number of licit (legal) analogs of fentanyl have also been developed. These include sufentanyl (Sufenta®), which is 20 to 40 times as potent as fentanyl; alfentanyl (Alfenta®), which is less potent than fentanyl but shorter acting (usually less than 15 minutes); and lofentanyl, which is about 60 times as potent as fentanyl and much longer lasting.

The opioid (morphine- and heroin-like) properties of fentanyl and its analogs have made these products very attractive to some recreational drug users. In some cases, drug dealers or users obtain fentanyl and its licit analogs by theft, fraudulent prescriptions, or illegal distribution by patients, physicians, and pharmacists for sale to drug users. In other cases, illicit analogs of fentanyl are manufactured and sold by dealers. Among the 10 or more illicit analogs that have been made are α-methyl fentanyl and 3-methyl fentanyl. All of these drugs mimic the psychoactive effects of morphine but are considerably more potent than the natural product. The analog 3-methyl fentanyl, for example, is about 3,000 times as potent as morphine itself.

Illicit analogs of fentanyl first became available in the mid-1970s. They appeared under the street names *China White* (a term originally used for a white powdery form of heroin imported from Southeast Asia) and "*synthetic heroin.*" The drugs are taken by injection, sniffed, or swallowed. They produce a strongly euphoric effect, similar to that obtained from heroin and morphine. As with all drugs, both licit and illicit, however, there are a number of risks involved in the use of fentanyl and its analogs. These risks include depression of the respiratory, circulatory, and central nervous systems; hypothermia (abnormally low body temperature); bradycardia (decrease in heart rate); hypotension (high blood pressure); and muscle weakness. Central nervous system effects can range from relatively mild conditions, such as disorientation, to very serious ones, including coma and death. Long-term effects of fentanyl analog overuse may include Parkinson-like neurological symptoms, such as uncontrollable tremors, drooling, impaired speech, paralysis, and irreversible brain damage. Fentanyl analogs are thought to have been responsible for more than 150 deaths since they were first introduced in the 1970s, and the U.S. Drug Enforcement Administration reported in 2004 that there had been 1,506 hospital emergency room cases related to misuse of fentanyl analogs.

Phenylethylamine Analogs

A second category of designer drugs can be classified as *phenylethylamines*. Members of this class of compounds contain three primary functional groups: the phenyl ($-C_6H_5$) group, ethyl ($-C_2H_5$) group, and amino ($-NH_2$) group. The phenylethylamines belong to the general class of arylalklyamines, which contain at least one aryl (derivatives of benzene and related compounds) group and at least one alkyl (derivatives of a saturated hydrocarbon) group. When the alkyl group is an ethyl (CH_3CH_2-) group, these compounds are known as *arylethylamines* or *arylethanamines*.

A number of very important natural and synthetic biochemicals belong to the phenylethylamine family. Two of these compounds, dopamine and epinephrine (adrenaline), are neurotransmitters, substances that carry chemical messages through the nervous system of humans and other animals. A third phenylethylamine, tyrosine, is an essential amino acid. And a familiar phenylethylamine found in plants is mescaline, whose chemical name is 2-(3,4,5-trimethoxyphenyl)ethylamine. The primary natural sources of mescaline are four varieties of cactus: two peyote species (*Lophophora williamsii* and *Lophophora diffusa*), the San Pedro cactus (*Trichocereus pachanoi*), and the Peruvian Torch cactus (*Trichocereus peruvianus*).

The first phenylethylamine of commercial significance to have been synthesized was amphetamine (1-phenyl-2-aminopropane or methylphenethylamine). Amphetamine was developed in 1887 by the Romanian chemist Lazar Edeleanu (1862–1941). For four decades, amphetamine was little more than a laboratory curiosity with no known pharmaceutical use. In 1927, however, the compound was found to have a number of physiological effects: It stimulates the central nervous system (CNS), increases blood pressure, and dilates nasal and bronchial passages. The last of these effects was responsible for its first commercial application, when in 1932 it was marketed under the trade name of Benzedrine® as a nonprescription inhaler for the treatment of nasal congestion.

One of the most interesting uses of amphetamine has been in the treatment of attention deficit hyperactivity disorder (ADHD). Individuals with this condition (usually children) display abnormally high levels of nervous activity that make it difficult for them to concentrate. Treatment with amphetamine—which normally *increases* CNS activity—tends to have the opposite effect in many ADHD individuals, however, reducing nervous activity and increasing the ability to focus on tasks. Amphetamine is no longer used as a nasal inhaler because of its toxic effects, but it still finds applications for use in weight-loss programs, relief of some nasal allergies, and the treatment of narcolepsy.

Methamphetamine

An analog of amphetamine called methamphetamine (1-phenyl-2-methylaminopropane or phenylisopropylmethylamine) was first synthesized in 1919 by the Japanese chemist Akira Ogata (1887–1978). Methamphetamine differs from amphetamine only in that a methyl group (-CH$_3$) replaces one of the amino hydrogens found in amphetamine. Methamphetamine occurs as a water-soluble white crystalline product suitable for administration by injection. It was originally marketed in the 1960s by Burroughs-Wellcome Pharmaceuticals under the trade name of Methedrine®. That trade name has to a considerable extent become a synonym for street versions of amphetamine available for recreational use. In 1935, a second analog of amphetamine was developed, dextroamphetamine, marketed as Dexedrine®. Dextroamphetamine has the same structural formula as amphetamine, except that it is an optical isomer of the original compound. (Optical isomers are two forms of a compound that differ from each other only in that their chemical structures are mirror images of each other.) It has uses similar to those of amphetamine and methamphetamine.

During World War II, the popularity of amphetamine and its analogs spread rapidly, less because of their originally intended medical benefits than because of their effects as CNS stimulants. The ability of these products to provide a quick burst of energy made them popular as weight-loss products, treatments for depression, and recreational drugs to provide an easy emotional "high." They became some of the original "uppers" so popular with the drug culture of the 1960s. The amphetamines are still widely used and known by names such as speed, uppers, pep pills, bennies, wake-ups, eye-openers, copilots, coast-to-coast, cartwheels, A's, black beauties, crank, meth, and crystal meth.

MDMA

By far the most important synthetic analog of amphetamine currently in illicit use is 3,4-methylenedioxymethamphetamine (MDMA). The formulas below show the close structural relationship of amphetamine, methamphetamine, and MDMA.

MDMA's history dates to the early years of the 20th century when researchers at the German pharmaceutical company Merck discovered the compound and a number of related amphetamine analogs, including 3,4-methylenedioxyamphetamine (MDA) and 3,4-methylenedioxy-N-ethylamphetamine (MDEA). Merck's research began as an attempt to discover a substance that could be used as a vasoconstrictor, a substance that causes a narrowing of blood vessels and can be used to reduce bleeding.

The first useful product discovered during this research was MDA, synthesized in 1910 by G. Mannish and W. Jacobsohn. Two years later, Mannish and Jacobsohn synthesized a second analog of amphetamine, MDMA. Merck saw no immediate uses for these new products at the time but patented them both for possible future applications.

In fact, no significant research was conducted on MDA and MDMA until nearly a half century later. By that time, researchers had begun to focus on possible psychoactive effects of the compounds. During the 1950s, the pharmaceutical firm of SmithKline French explored the possibility of using MDA as an antidepressant and tranquilizer.

Although they obtained patents on the use of MDA for these applications (and also as a weight-loss product), they never developed commercial products from the compound. The problem, which appeared during human trials, was that the psychic effects on subjects were too severe to permit use of MDA for its intended functions. The compound caused overstimulation of the CNS, which sometimes resulted in panic attacks among subjects. This drawback did not, however, prevent the spread of MDA in the illicit drug market, where it eventually became one of the most popular substances used in the 1960s, when it was widely known as "the love drug."

Merck researchers first reported the synthesis of MDMA in 1912. The company obtained a patent for the compound two years later, although at the time it had no specific application in mind for the compound. Like MDA, MDMA was essentially "left on the shelf" until the 1950s, when animal studies on the compound were conducted

© Infobase Publishing

Chemical structures of amphetamine, methamphetamine, and MDMA for the U.S. Central Intelligence Agency (CIA) at the U.S. Army's Edgewood Arsenal in Maryland. Researchers were interested in the possibility of using MDMA as a mind-altering drug that could be employed for brainwashing or espionage activities. Unlike another drug being tested at the time, lysergic acid diethylamide (LSD), MDMA was not tested on human subjects, and military research on MDMA largely came to a dead end.

By the late 1960s, a handful of individual researchers began to synthesize MDMA and to study its psychoactive properties, exploring possible applications for the treatment of mental and emotional disorders. One of the first, and probably most famous, of these investigators was Alexander Shulgin, professor of chemistry at San Francisco State University. Shulgin tested the effects of MDMA on himself and later wrote the first scholarly paper on the compound and its psychoactive effects, "The psychotomimetic properties of 3,4,5-trimethoxyamphetamine," published in the journal *Nature* in 1961 (with S. Bunnell and T. Sargent).

Over the past four decades, Shulgin has written extensively, both for scholarly publications and for general readers, about the psychoactive effects of MDMA and a number of other drugs. In laboratory notes from September 1976, for example, he reported on one experience with MDMA. "I feel absolutely clean inside," he wrote, "and there is nothing but pure euphoria. I have never felt so great or believed this to be possible. The cleanliness, clarity, and marvelous feeling of solid inner strength continued throughout the rest of the day and evening. I am overcome by the profundity of the experience." Shulgin was excited about the possible application of MDMA and other psychoactive drugs for the treatment of mental and emotional disorders. In a 1978 book, he wrote that these drugs might provide patients with "an easily controlled altered state of consciousness with emotional and sensual overtones."

News of Shulgin's research soon spread among psychotherapists, who saw the potential for using MDMA as a tool for patient counseling. In less than a decade, more than 1,000 psychotherapists were using the drug with their patients. MDMA by this time had become widely known as *Adam* because of its tendency to create within patients a certain naive innocence that one associates with the first human, and for some patients, the drug proved to be highly effective, causing them, according to one commentator, to feel "truly well for the first time in their lives."

As MDMA was being adopted by professional therapists, however, it was also becoming known to users of recreational drugs. Word of its psychoactive effects gradually began to circulate among illegal drug users and by 1977 it was being manufactured by amateur chemists and sold on the street for recreational use. Four years later, MDMA had been given its now-most-popular street name, "*Ecstasy*," by some unknown drug dealer. The name appears to have been chosen because of the compound's ability to produce feelings of bliss, euphoria, exhilaration, and rapture.

MDMA's potential to harm users soon became a matter of concern to at least some governmental and law enforcement officials. It was banned almost immediately in the United Kingdom where it was categorized as a Class A drug (comparable to a Schedule I drug in the United States) under the nation's Misuse of Drugs Act. Other amphetamine analogs, such as MDA and MDE, were also included in the Class A listing.

Similar action in the United States occurred more slowly, at least partly because of the relative paucity of reports of MDMA-related health effects in this country. According to the Drug Abuse Warning Network (DAWN), operated by the U.S. Department of Health and Human Services' Substance Abuse and Mental Health Services Administration (SAMHSA), only eight individuals sought emergency room treatment for MDMA events between 1977 and 1985. Still, by the end of that period, the Drug Enforcement Administration (DEA) had decided to classify MDMA, MDA, MDE, and related compounds as Schedule I drugs. Except for a brief period between December 1987 and March 1988, when the drugs were declassified for technical reasons, they have continued to be listed as Schedule I drugs. Today, 10 phenylethylamines are listed as Schedule I drugs. In addition to mescaline, MDA, MDMA, and MDE, they include 4-bromo-2,5-dimethoxyamphetamine (DOB); 2,5-dimethoxyamphetamine (DMA); 4-methoxyamphetamine (PMA); 5-methoxy-3,4-methylenedioxyamphetamine (MMDA); 4-methyl-2,5-dimethoxyamphetamine (DOM, STP); and 3,4,5-trimethoxyamphetamine (TMA).

◄ ALEXANDER "SASHA" SHULGIN (1925—   ) ►

Perhaps the best known advocate of designer drugs within the scientific community is Alexander "Sasha" Shulgin. For nearly 50 years, Shulgin has been synthesizing, analyzing, experimenting with, and reporting on the effects of a host of designer drugs on the human body and emotions.

Alexander Shulgin was born in Berkeley, California, on June 17, 1925. Like many other boys of the time, he had a home chemistry set, which he used in the basement of his house, and he developed a passion for chemistry early in his life. After graduating from high school at the age of 16, he entered Harvard University on a full scholarship. His academic career was cut short by World War II, when he left Harvard to join the U.S. Navy. After the war, he returned to the University of California at Berkeley to complete his studies, earning first his bachelor's degree, and then his Ph.D. in biochemistry in 1954. He then pursued a postdoctoral program in psychiatry and pharmacology at the University of California at San Francisco (UCSF) before accepting a position as senior research chemist at the Dow Chemical Company.

Shulgin's most significant accomplishment at Dow was to develop a pesticide known as physostigmine, a substance that was to become one of Dow's best-selling products. In appreciation of Shulgin's work, Dow provided him with a laboratory of his own where he was allowed to work on projects that were of special interest to him. One of those projects turned out to be the synthesis and study of psychedelic compounds.

According to Shulgin, his passion for the study of psychedelics emerged after the first time he took mescaline in 1960. He says that he saw the world in a new and dramatically different way that inspired in him a "burning desire" to understand more about the chemical nature of compounds that could produce such profound experiences. As a result of the mescaline experience, he told an interviewer from *Playboy* magazine in 2004, "I had found my learning path," the direction in which he wanted the rest of his career to go.

In 1965, Shulgin decided to leave Dow to pursue medical studies at UCSF. After two years in the program, however, he decided that he preferred to continue his work with psychedelics and left UCSF to become an independent consultant on psychedelic drugs. That decision brought Shulgin and the Drug Enforcement Administration (DEA) into a highly unusual relationship. Although the DEA's job is to discourage the development and study of illegal drugs in almost any respect, the agency and Shulgin worked out a working understanding that allowed the chemist to synthesize and study a number of otherwise illicit or unapproved drugs with the provision that they not be sold or otherwise be made available to anyone outside of his own laboratory. That relationship worked well for both parties for many years, even resulting in the publication of a handbook on the Controlled Substances Act, written by Shulgin, that became a standard reference for DEA employees.

In addition to his extensive freelance work on psychedelic compounds, Shulgin has also served as a member of the faculty at San Francisco State University and the University of California at Berkeley. He is perhaps best known to the general public as the author, with his wife Ann, of two books on psychedelic drugs, *PiHKAL* (*Phenethylamines I Have Known and Loved: A Chemical Love Story*), and *TiHKAL* (*Tryptamines I Have Known and Loved: The Chemistry Continues*). The two books provide not only a fascinating autobiographical sketch of the authors' lives and works but a detailed introduction to the chemical synthesis, characterization, and properties of the chemicals belonging to major psychedelic families, the phenylethylamines and the tryptamines.

Shulgin is one of a handful of prominent scientists who has chosen to carry out research on chemical compounds with psychedelic effects. Those scientists walk a thin line between legitimate scientific experimentation that is generally recognized as valid and useful within the scientific community and the investigation of drugs that is, if not actually illicit, of questionable legal status. They pursue their studies because they think they can learn about chemical compounds that may produce altered states of consciousness and new ways of thinking and feeling that may bring relief and solace to individuals with a host of mental and emotional problems as well as opportunities for ordinary individuals who are eager to explore new ways of looking at the world. Critics of this research argue that these investigations are more likely to result in a host of physical, mental, and emotional problems among the people who use them, problems that can result in long-term health problems and even death. For half a century, Shulgin has maintained his passion for the study of psychedelic drugs and sharing the information he has learned with the community at large.

As is always the case, classification as Schedule I drugs has by no means prevented the production, sale, and use of phenylethylamines, and drug overdose and death sometimes result from such use. As shown in the graph below, the number of deaths reported from MDMA, for example, rose from one in 1994 to somewhat less than 100 in 2001, the last year for which data are available. Over the same period, the number of emergency room admissions attributed to MDMA abuse rose from 421 to 4,026, an increase of 856 percent. To put this number in perspective, note that the number of emergency room admissions attributed to cocaine use during this period increased from 135,711 to 199,198 (an increase of 47 percent); the number admitted due to use of amphetamines increased from 9,581 to 21,644 (an increase of 126 percent); and the number admitted due to heroin use increased from 69,556 to 93,519 (an increase of 34 percent). Surveys show that MDMA remains one of the most popular illegal drugs in the United States and is often the drug of choice at raves. In a 2001 survey conducted by the National Institute

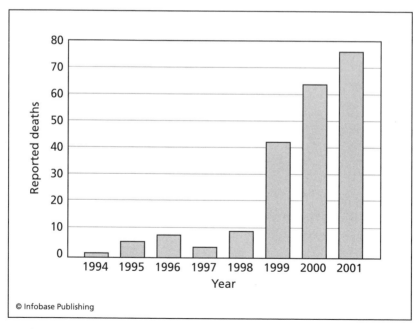

© Infobase Publishing

Number of deaths resulting from MDMA use, 1994–2001

on Drug Abuse, for example, 9.2 percent of 12th graders interviewed reported that they had used MDMA at least once in the previous year, as did 6.2 percent of all 10th graders and 3.5 percent of all 8th graders interviewed.

The psychoactive effects of MDMA have now been well studied. For most people, in moderate amounts the drug produces feelings of euphoria and well-being that last anywhere from six to 24 hours. For some individuals, in larger doses, and/or over extended periods of use, however, a number of unpleasant and potentially dangerous side effects have been reported. These effects include headaches, nausea, vomiting, blurred vision, jaw clenching, and increased heart rate and blood pressure. In the most severe instances, there may be convulsions, anxiety attacks, seizures, brain damage, and death.

The neurochemical basis for these effects has also been studied in some detail. Researchers have learned that MDMA (and its phenyl-ethylamine cousins) interferes with the normal function of at least two neurotransmitters in the brain, serotonin and dopamine. Under normal circumstances, nerve messages are transmitted through the CNS when an axon on one neuron releases a neurotransmitter, such as serotonin or dopamine, which travels across the synapse between two neurons and is taken up at a receptor site in the second neuron.

MDMA and, presumably, other phenylethylamines seem to interfere with this process in at least three ways. First, they may stimulate the release of the neurotransmitter, resulting in an increased concentration of serotonin or dopamine in the synapse, amplifying the stimulatory effect of these compounds on the CNS. Second, phenylethylamines may block the receptor sites in a neuron, preventing the absorption of serotonin or dopamine, again resulting in an increase in concentration of the neurotransmitter that remains in circulation in the CNS. Third, the presence of a phenylethylamine may actually cause a decrease in the amount of serotonin or dopamine available for nerve transmission, resulting in a (sometimes dramatic) decrease in CNS activity that can be associated with some of the more dangerous side effects of the drug's use.

Studies on the effects of MDMA on the structure and function of neurons have been conducted in monkeys. Those studies show that MDMA may cause structural changes in neurons like those

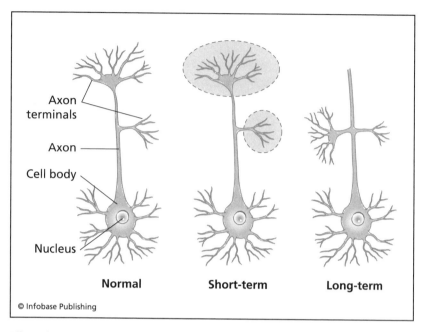

Effect of MDMA on serotonin neurons in monkey brain

illustrated in the diagram above that could be responsible for changes in neurotransmitter production. Since these changes were produced by relatively large doses of the drug (two times a day for four days) on experimental animals, comparable effects on the human brain of other amounts of the drug are not clear. Consensus within the scientific community appears to be, however, that MDMA poses potentially serious threats to the human CNS and other body systems in both the short and long term.

Meperidine Analogs

The third major category of designer drugs includes analogs of the compound meperidine (pethidine; 1-methyl-4-phenyl-4-piperidine-carboxylic acid ethyl ester). Meperidine was first synthesized in 1937 by two biochemists, Otto Eisleb and Otto Schaumann, employed by the German chemical firm of Farbwerke Hoechst. The firm later patented the drug under the trade name of Dolantin® and it has become available in other nations under other trade names, including Pethidine®, Demerol®, Centralgin®, and Meperidin®. The compound is widely used for a variety of purposes, including the relief of moderate to severe pain and as a support for general anesthesia. Meperidine is currently classified as a Schedule II drug under the Controlled Substances Act, meaning that it has a high potential for abuse as well as valid medical applications.

The two most common analogs of meperidine used as recreational drugs are 1-methyl-4-phenyl-4-propionoxypiperidine (MPPP) and 1-[2-phenylethyl]-4-acetyloxypiperdine (PEPAP). These compounds have a number of street names, including new heroin, synthetic heroin, synthetic Demerol, and China White. MPPP and PEPAP have pharmacological effects similar to those of heroin, but more pronounced, producing a sense of euphoria and release from the real world. MPPP, for example, is three times as potent has heroin.

Of the two analogs, MPPP poses a somewhat more serious threat to users because a highly toxic by-product, 1-methyl-4-phenyl-1,2,5,6-tetrahydropyridine (MPTP), is sometimes formed during its synthesis. MPTP forms during the synthesis of MPPP if the pH of the reaction solution is too low or the reaction temperature is too high. Thus, errors that might appear relatively minor to an inexperienced chemist can result in a contaminated product (MPPP + MPTP) that is highly toxic to users.

The toxicology of MPTP has been extensively studied in experimental animals, and there is substantial evidence that the compound is toxic to neurons in the brain that produce dopamine, an essential neurotransmitter. Circumstantial evidence obtained from studies of humans who have ingested MPTP support this conclusion. Such individuals typically pass through a series of stages that mimic the development of Parkinson's disease, chiefly an affliction of the elderly. Scientists now know that Parkinson's is caused by a deficiency of dopamine in the brain. Symptoms of the earliest stage of both Parkinson's and MPTP poisoning include difficulty in speaking, blurred vision, "nodding off," drooling, intermittent tremors, disorientation, and hallucinations. A second stage, which occurs a few days after ingestion of contaminated MPPP, is characterized by an increase in muscular rigidity so that a person tends to "freeze up" suddenly and becomes unable to move. These symptoms appear to be irreversible and lead eventually to classic end-stage Parkinson symptoms such as inability to maintain one's posture, extensive tremors, muscular rigidity, a fixed stare, and, eventually, death. This syndrome was first reported in 1979 when a 23-year-old graduate student accidentally produced MPTP in his laboratory, tried the drug, and eventually died from what later appeared to be MPTP poisoning.

The incidence of drug abuse related to the meperidine analogs is relatively modest compared with that of painkillers available to drug abusers. For example, the number of emergency room cases involving meperidine and its analogs has stayed relatively constant over the past decade, ranging from a low of 730 cases in 1998 to a high of 1,085 cases in 2000. Despite these low numbers, the dramatic physiological effects associated with the use of meperidine analogs is sufficient to cause some alarm about the risks of these drugs.

Phencyclidine Analogs

A fourth major category of designer drugs includes phencyclidine and its analogs. Phencyclidine (1-phenylcyclohexylpiperidine; PCP) belongs to the arylhexylamines, a family of chemical compounds that contain one or more six-membered rings attached to a central nitrogen atom. This family of drugs has been assigned a special place in the study of drug abuse because of the highly unusual, even bizarre, effects they have on at least some drug users—even compared with those of other illicit drugs.

PCP was first synthesized in 1926 by two German chemists, A. Kötz and P. J. Merkel. As with so many other drugs, no practical use was found for the compound for some time. Then, in the 1950s, the Parke-Davis pharmaceutical company began exploring the use of PCP as an anesthetic for humans. The compound showed promise for this application because of its ability to make subjects unaware of pain, a phenomenon known as *dissociative anesthesia.* In spite of some troublesome side effects with its use, PCP was patented by Parke-Davis in 1963 and made available as a surgical anesthetic under the trade name of Sernyl®. After only two years of use, however, Sernyl® was withdrawn from the marketplace because of the same side effects observed during testing: disorientation, delirium, and hallucinations. In 1967, PCP was reintroduced as an anesthetic but was limited to veterinary applications.

Just as PCP was reentering the marketplace as a veterinary anesthetic, it also began to appear on the streets as a new recreational drug. The compound appealed to users because of its ability to produce a sense of euphoria accompanied by some of the more pleasant sensations associated with alcoholic inebriation. It became known by street names such as angel dust, hog, superweed, THC, ozone, wack, and rocket fuel. The drug produces a rather wide variety of fairly bizarre side effects that include a general numbness that spreads throughout the body, enhanced sensations, impaired perceptions, panic reactions, violent behaviors, paranoia, hallucinations, and psychotic reactions similar to those experienced with schizophrenia. Overdoses of the drug may result in cardiac arrhythmia, seizures, muscular rigidity, acute renal (kidney) failure, coma, and death.

Because of its potential dangers, PCP was classified as a Schedule III drug in the early 1970s and advanced to a Schedule II drug in 1978. Today, a number of PCP analogs have been produced, and all are listed as either Schedule I or Schedule II drugs. Some examples of these analogs are 1-phenylcyclohexylamine (Schedule II), 1-piperidinocyclohexanecarbonitrile (PCC; Schedule II), N-ethyl-1-phenylcyclohexylamine (PCE; Schedule I), 1-(1-phenyl- cyclohexyl)-pyrrolidine (PCPy or PHP; Schedule II), and 1-(1-(2-thienyl-cyclohexyl)-piperdine (TPCP or TCP; Schedule I).

According to SAMHSA surveys, PCP is not particularly popular as a recreational drug among high school students. In its most recent survey (2003), the agency reported that the percentage of 12th grade students who reported having used PCP at any time in their lives ranged from a low of 2.7 percent in 1995 to a high of 4.0 percent a year later, with an average rate of use at about 3.0 percent for the years 1991 through 2003.

A PCP analog that has raised increasing concern in recent years is ketamine (2-(methylamino)-2-(2-chlorophenyl)-cyclohexanone). Ketamine was first synthesized in 1962 at Parke-Davis Laboratories by Calvin Stevens, who was searching for a PCP-like substance that could be used as a human anesthetic. At first, ketamine appeared to satisfy this condition very satisfactorily since it produces a state of unconsciousness without significantly affecting a person's respiration or circulation. It promised, therefore, to qualify as a low-risk anesthetic for surgical procedures on humans, and it became available for use by the medical community in the late 1960s. The compound is still used in some parts of the world for that purpose, and it is available without prescription in a few countries, such as Mexico.

Concerns about the use of ketamine as a human anesthetic began to arise in the early 1970s, however, when some patients reported having unsettling psychedelic experiences. Over the next two decades, the use of ketamine in surgical procedures in the United States decreased until, in 1999, the DEA listed ketamine as a Schedule III drug. It is now used almost exclusively in the United States for veterinary procedures, although it can be used for certain specialized procedures with humans.

Almost since its discovery, ketamine has also been used as a recreational drug for people seeking "out-of-body" experiences. In limited doses, the drug produces a "rush" that is followed by a far more relaxed, dreamy feeling resembling mild alcoholic intoxication. The drug affects most of the senses, resulting in blurred vision, diminished ability to hear sounds, clumsiness in movement, and general lack of coordination. In larger doses, these conditions become more severe, eventually resulting in confusion, disorientation, difficulty in moving, loss of speech, hallucinations, and near-death experiences (NDE), in which one is certain that he or she is about to die.

Deaths attributable to ketamine appear to be extremely rare, if not actually nonexistent. The drug also appears to be relatively low in popularity, compared to other "club drugs" such as MDMA, methamphetamine, and LSD. The number of emergency room visits attributed to ketamine use has varied considerably over the last decade, ranging from 19 in 1994 to 396 in 1999 to 679 in 2001 to 260 in 2002, the last date for which data are available.

GHB and Rohypnol

The preceding four classes of drugs by no means exhaust the repertoire of chemical compounds available to illegal drug users. Two additional substances commonly used as recreational drugs today include gamma hydroxybutyric acid (or gamma hydroxybutyrate; GHB) and Rohypnol (flunitrazepam).

GHB is a naturally occurring compound found in every cell of mammals. It occurs in greatest concentrations in the heart, kidney, and skeletal muscles. GHB is chemically related to gamma amino-butyric acid (GABA), a well-known neurotransmitter, and is thought by some researchers to itself act as a neurotransmitter in some parts of the CNS.

GHB was first synthesized in the laboratory by the French bio-chemist Henri Laborit (1914–1995) in 1961. In the succeeding four decades, extensive research has been conducted on the pharma-cological uses and effects of GHB. In general, those studies appear to suggest that GHB has some valuable applications in the medical sciences. It functions well as an anesthetic with apparently few or no serious side effects. Based on this research, the drug has been adopted in many parts of the world for use as a general anesthetic, a treatment for narcolepsy and insomnia, a treatment for alcoholism, and an aid in childbirth.

GHB has met a somewhat different fate in the United States, how-ever. In 1990, the FDA banned the sale of the drug in the United States because of its concerns over possible risks to human health. In view of the generally positive research on the drug's use, the sci-entific basis of the FDA's decision was not entirely clear at the time to some observers. In any case, the drug's legal status was clarified in 2000 when the DEA classified it as a Schedule I drug under the Controlled Substances Act.

GHB continues to have some popularity within the drug culture, however, and among bodybuilders and other athletes, for the latter group because of its ability to stimulate muscle growth. Known by a variety of street names, such as liquid X, liquid E, gamma-oh!, goop, Georgia home boy, and grievous bodily harm, GHB acts much like alcohol, making a user feel relaxed, happy, and sociable. Increased doses produce effects similar to those of alcoholic intoxication, in-cluding sleepiness, disorientation, dizziness, lack of coordination, nausea, and vomiting.

The line between pleasurable relaxation and dangerous overin-toxication is, unfortunately, very narrow. Consumption of no more than a few grams of GHB can result in a serious condition known as *temporary unrousable unconsciousness,* a type of coma that can be life-threatening. The likelihood of its occurrence is increased by two factors. First, GHB users often combine the drug with alcohol, which seriously amplifies GHB's effects on the body. Second, GHB is most commonly made available as an aqueous solution of unknowable (to the user) concentration, making it impossible for a person to monitor the amount of the drug ingested.

The number of deaths from GHB overdoses in the United States has been relatively small, amounting to fewer than 75 between 1994 and 2003. During the same period, trends in emergency room cases attributed to GHB overdose have varied from a low of 56 in 1994 to a high of 4,969 in 2000. In the two most recent years for which data were available, the number of such cases had dropped to 3,340 in 2001 and 3,330 in 2002.

Some analogs of GHB are also available on the street. These include gamma hydroxyvalerate (GHV), gamma butyrolactone (GBL), gamma valerolactone (GVL), and 1,4-butanediol. The last three of these drugs all metabolize into GHB, so they have effects similar to those of GHB itself. None of the four analogs of GHB has yet been classified by the DEA in any one of the five schedules defined by the Controlled Substances Act.

Flunitrazepam is a member of the benzodiazepine family, a group of compounds that contain two functional groups in common, the benzo and diazepine groups (as their name suggests). The family includes a number of popular drugs prescribed primarily for the treatment of insomnia and anxiety, such as estazolam (ProSom®), flurazepam (Dalmane®), temazepam (Restoril®), triazolam (Halcion®), alprazolam (Xanax®), chlordiazepoxide (Librium®), clorazepate (Tranxene®), diazepam (Valium®), halazepam (Paxipam®), lorzepam (Ativan®), oxazepam (Serax®), prazepam (Centrax®), and quazepam (Doral®). The benzodiazepines are among the most frequently prescribed drugs in the United States. Flunitrazepam is marketed by the Hoffman-LaRoche pharmaceutical company under the trade name of Rohypnol®. It is known by a variety of street names, such as roofies, Mexican valium, R-2, ropies, circles, and rib.

Rohypnol® is legally available in many parts of the world, including Europe and South America, where it is used as a preanesthetic sedative and for the treatment of insomnia and narcolepsy. The drug has not, however, been approved for use in the United States, so it is not legally available in this country. Nevertheless, a substantial illegal trade in Rohypnol® has existed for many years, and tens of thousands of pills are imported into the country annually. According to an annual study conducted by the National Institute on Drug Abuse, 1.6 percent of all 12th graders surveyed in 2002 reported that they had used Rohypnol® at least once in the previous year. Only 0.7 percent of 10th graders and 0.3 percent of 8th graders reported such use.

Physiological effects of Rohypnol® are similar to those experienced with other sedatives and anesthetics and include drowsiness, dizziness, lack of coordination, confusion, decreased blood pressure, respiratory depression, nausea, and vomiting. Increased dosages can result in blackouts that may include partial amnesia.

One of the greatest concerns related to the use of Rohypnol® has been its potential as a date rape drug. When mixed with alcohol, its effects are substantially amplified, significantly decreasing a person's ability to evaluate and resist aggressive actions by another person. Although the problem of date rape involving Rohypnol® has been extensively discussed in recent years, reliable data on its actual extent have been difficult to obtain.

Guesses and Risks

The history of designer drugs provides an intriguing lesson about the process by which new drugs—both licit and illicit—are developed and the legal issues involved in their eventual approval or ban. Traditionally, chemists have begun their search for new

Rohypnol® is approved for medical use in many parts of the world, but not in the United States. (Garo/Photo Researchers, Inc.)

drugs either with plant or mineral compounds found in nature or with synthetic chemicals known to have some desirable pharmacological effect on humans. They have then modified the chemical structure of these compounds—adding a methyl or a hydroxyl group here, inserting a ring system, or making some other molecular change—to see what new effects, if any, appear.

The fundamental problem with this approach is that the likelihood of their success cannot be reliably predicted. Even in compounds that otherwise appear to be similar to existing and effective substances, changes such as methylation, deamination, or arylation may or may not produce the same pharmacological effect—or *any* pharmacological effect. Inventing new drugs by manipulating molecular structure is still largely a trial-and-error procedure.

An additional twist to this story is that, as demonstrated in this chapter, one need not be employed by a large pharmaceutical firm in order to get into the business of new drug synthesis. Many individuals with a rudimentary knowledge of chemistry synthesize analogs of existing drugs that may not be legally available to the general public. The whole business of designer drugs is, of course, based on the premise that someone somewhere has been able to synthesize a chemical compound that produces certain psychopharmacological effects that at least some people want to experience, but that are not available from *legal* drugs. Chemists who can achieve this objective can become hugely wealthy.

The business of designer drugs is, in some ways, like an arms race between governmental agencies such as the Food and Drug Administration and the Drug Enforcement Administration, whose job it is to protect the general public from potentially harmful consumer products, and chemists who are constantly looking for the next new psychoactive drug that will avoid existing regulations and, therefore, be legal to sell, at least for some period of time.

Finally, designer drugs pose an interesting issue for those individuals who decide to make recreational drug use a part of their lives. Without question, many such individuals use Ecstasy, roofies, vitamin K, and other illegal drugs without experiencing any serious long-term effects. By their very nature, however, designer drugs pose a frightening fundamental risk. Because they are generally produced by unmonitored, often amateur, operations, they may contain impurities (such as MPTP) whose health effects are far more serious than those of the pure drug itself. Choosing to use a recreational drug, then, involves not only a decision to experience some new and perhaps exciting psychic experience but also a choice to put one's life at risk in having that experience.

5
RATIONAL DRUG DESIGN
STRUCTURE-ACTIVITY RELATIONSHIPS AND COMBINATORIAL CHEMISTRY

D o you like to gamble? Is a toss of the dice or the spin of a slot machine enough to get your blood rushing? If so, we have a great game for you: Betting on new drugs. All that is needed to play this game is a few million dollars to invest, the patience to wait up to 10 years to find out if you have won or not, and the willingness to take odds of about 1,000 to 1 for your winning the bet. How is that for a gamble?

Obviously, betting on drug development is not a form of gambling in which the players are individuals. Only large corporations with substantial financial assets can take this level of risk, and they do so for two major reasons. One reason, of course, is the opportunity of providing people with new chemical compounds that will ease pain, extend life, cure disease, and improve life in other ways. The other reason is that a successful new drug can result in very large profits for the company that has gambled on its development. For example, sales of the cholesterol-reducing drug Lipitor® earns its parent company, Pfizer, Inc., about $10 billion annually.

Lipitor®, however, is the exception. Only about one compound out of 5,000 that starts the drug development process ever makes it through and is approved for use, and "scoring big" with a totally new drug such as Lipitor® is a rare event. In 2003, for example, the FDA approved 466 new and generic drugs and biologic products for sale in the United States, but only 21 of those were entirely new drugs—called new molecular entities (NME)—with active ingredients that had never before been marketed in the United States. Since each compound that successfully passes through the drug approval process is estimated to cost anywhere from $900 million to $1.7 billion, pharmaceutical companies are continuously engaged in a tight gamble to earn back the money they invest in the overall drug development process.

Steps in the Development of a New Drug

The drug development process involves two major steps. In the first step, researchers look for chemical compounds, known as *lead compounds,* that are promising candidates for new and useful drugs. In the second step, those lead compounds and their chemical analogs are subjected to an exhaustive program of testing, first with experimental animals and then with human subjects. The purpose of those testing programs is twofold: first, to ensure that the compound being tested is safe for use in humans and/or other animals, and second, to determine that it is efficacious—that is, that it produces some desirable biological effect.

Traditionally, lead compounds have been discovered in one of two ways. The first is one of trial and error. This is the way many plant and animal products and minerals have been found to be effective in the treatment of some medical disorder. For example, no one knows when the first person learned that chewing on the bark of the willow tree (*Salix alba*) helped relieve pain and reduce fever, but willow bark has been used in many cultures for untold centuries for just that purpose. Today we know that the active ingredient in willow bark is a derivative of salicylic acid ($C_6H_4(OH)COOH$), which today is sold commercially as aspirin or one of its analogs. Drug researchers continue to rely heavily on the study of folk medicines—a science known as *ethnopharmacology*—for the discovery of new plant and animal products that may have medical applications in the modern world. Indeed, scientists have discovered that the medical profession has a great deal to learn from so-called primitive cultures in terms of the materials that can be used to treat pain and disease.

The second source of lead compounds has been serendipity: the fortunate but unexpected discovery that a particular chemical compound is efficacious in the treatment of some disease. Perhaps the most famous of such discoveries was that made by Sir Alexander Fleming (1881–1955) who, in the 1920s, accidentally discovered that a fungus growing in his laboratory—*Penicillium notatum*—was capable of killing bacteria. The active ingredient extracted from that fungus was given the name of *penicillin*. Penicillin was one of the first commercially successful antibiotics.

Indeed, the science of antibiotics itself originally grew not out of research on drugs and disease but out of the dye industry in Germany. As early as the first decade of the 20th century, the German bacteriologist Paul Ehrlich (1854–1915) suggested that compounds originally developed as dyes might be effective in killing bacteria and other disease-causing agents. The first success of his research along these lines was the discovery that a dye called trypan red was able to kill the protozoa that cause the disease trypanosomiasis and related infections.

Ehrlich's research was continued by a number of his colleagues and successors. In the 1920s, for example, the German chemist Gerhard Domagk (1895–1964) discovered that a compound originally developed for dyeing leather, prontosil red, protected experimental animals from certain types of infections caused by members of the staphylococcus and streptococcus families. Domagk eventually found that the antibacterial action of the dye was caused by one of its metabolites, a compound known as sulfanilamide.

The discoveries of penicillin and prontosil were important in the history of drug design for another reason. In both cases, chemists reasoned that chemical compounds *similar* to those that had already been found to be effective in the treatment of a disease (such as penicillin or prontosil) might also be efficacious as drugs. To test this hypothesis, they synthesized a number of analogs of successful drugs, sometimes with spectacular success. In the case of penicillin, for example, analog synthesis produced a whole family of drugs structurally related to the compound originally discovered by

Fleming, each with a specific application of its own. Many of these penicillin analogs are still in use today.

Similar success was achieved in the synthesis of analogs of prontosil and sulfanilamide. A number of these analogs were prepared and tested and found to be effective against a variety of infectious diseases.

Trial and error and serendipity continue to play major roles in the development of new drugs. As mentioned in earlier chapters, the search for new natural products to use as drugs, the use of recombinant DNA, and the design of analogs of existing drugs all involve some degree of chance in that scientists never know with certainty what compounds will have desirable pharmacological properties. Serendipity, by its very nature, will always account for the discovery of some new drugs. These techniques are still relevant to drug development, that is, even though they always involve a significant degree of gamble.

In recent decades, however, researchers have begun to rely on less chancy approaches to the development of new drugs. They have tried to develop more rational techniques in which the direction of research and development is based on concrete and specific knowledge about the molecular structure of chemical compounds that have a high probability of possessing desirable pharmacological effects. This approach to drug development is called rational drug design.

Rational Drug Design

Rational drug design is a technique of drug development that is based on one of two fundamental approaches. The first approach assumes that a compound that has been shown to be efficacious as a drug in the past can probably be modified in a number of ways that will produce analogs, some of which may also be effective as drugs. This approach is not so different in principle from that used by researchers who developed analogs of penicillin and sulfanilamide. However, theoretical understanding of the kinds of change that can be made in a molecule and the effects those changes are likely to have on a compound's biological activity have advanced significantly. Consequently, analog variety has vastly increased. More than 10,000 analogs of sulfanilamide, for example, have now been synthesized and tested.

The second approach is based on studies of the target of a drug—for instance, an enzyme responsible for a medical malfunction or some portion of a microorganism that causes a disease. By understanding the chemical structure of the enzyme or the microorganism and the way in which it behaves chemically, the drug researcher hopes to be able to develop an agent that will interfere with the enzyme or microorganism's action, preventing the medical problem.

Rational drug design has become possible only recently because of the availability of detailed crystallographic structures of target molecules. Researchers can now see with clarity the shape of receptor sites into which drug molecules must fit if they are to exert their pharmacological effects. This knowledge, in theory, makes it possible for them to design new drug molecules that have predictable effects on those receptor sites.

Unfortunately, this capability has not been translated into practical results as quickly and as easily as one might have hoped. A number of practical problems have arisen in converting knowledge about molecular shape into the development of new drugs. For example, the process by which a drug molecule docks at a receptor site is always a dynamic operation that is not easily modeled by a static three-dimensional crystal model, no matter how detailed and accurate it is. As a result, rational drug design has thus far resulted in the synthesis of very large numbers of possible drug molecules on which testing has taken place only very slowly. Very few successful products have worked their way through the testing pipeline at this point, and rational drug design is still in its earliest stages of development. The rest of this section is devoted to a discussion of the principles and techniques on which rational drug design is based.

Structure-Activity Relationships

Rational drug design is based on a fundamental concept, namely the assumption that the biological effects produced by a specific chemical compound are largely determined by that compound's molecular structure. That is, the three-dimensional structure of a chemical molecule determines the way in which that molecule reacts with other molecules in living systems and, hence, is responsible for its biological effects. The term *structure-activity relationship* (SAR) is commonly used to express this concept.

One of the earliest, simplest, and best-known examples of this concept is the lock-and-key model of enzyme action first proposed by German chemist Emil Fischer (1852–1919) in 1894. While it has been significantly modified since that time, the general mode of action suggested by Fischer is probably generally correct for most types of enzyme action. According to the lock-and-key model, illustrated below,

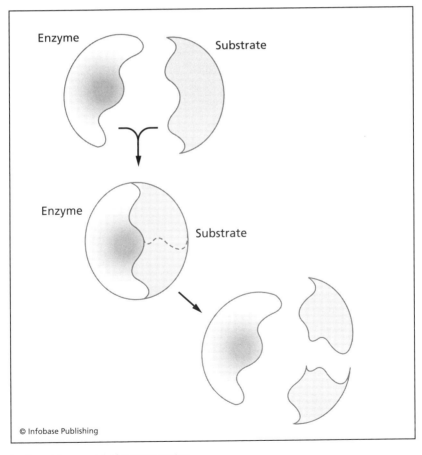

© Infobase Publishing

Lock-and-key model of enzyme action

an enzyme and its corresponding *substrate* (the molecule on which it acts) are compatible with each other if, and only if, the molecular structures of the two entities match each other very closely. In such cases, the enzyme slides into place in an opening in the substrate and forms bonds with its target in at least one (and usually more than one) position. Any of a variety of chemical changes within the substrate then takes place, producing one or more new substances, and the enzyme is released from its connection to the substrate.

This explanation of enzyme action is helpful, but far from complete. For one thing, enzymes differ significantly in the ways that they interact with other compounds. Some enzymes bond and react with only specific compounds, while others bond and react with an array of compounds in a chemical family that have the same or similar functional groups. Some enzymes fit neatly into an opening in a substrate, while others actually change the shape of the substrate on which they operate. The fact that enzyme actions are so diverse simply confirms that the chemical structures of enzymes and substrates differ significantly, and the chemical mechanisms by which they interact can be very complex indeed. In fact, the tools needed to understand the precise molecular shapes of enzymes and substrates have become available only recently. Once these shapes have become known, scientists are able to unravel the exact steps that take place when enzyme and substrate interact with each other.

Pharmacological research has also benefited from the development of sophisticated tools because they have made it possible for researchers to determine the exact molecular structure of compounds involved in the disease process. With this information, they can devise molecules that bond with and inactivate those compounds (just as enzymes bond with substrates). Consider just one example of this process: the development of a drug to treat human immunodeficiency virus (HIV) infection.

Acquired immunodeficiency syndrome (AIDS), the disease caused by HIV, was first discovered in the 1980s, and its rapid spread and terrible effects on human populations are now well known. During the 1990s, researchers launched one of the largest and most aggressive research programs in the history of medicine to find ways of dealing with this disease. An essential part of that program was an exhaustive study of the agent responsible for the disease, the human immunodeficiency virus (HIV). Today, the chemical structure and biological function of this agent are as well known as virtually any other disease-causing agent ever discovered.

Early in the effort to develop a drug to treat HIV infection, researchers found that the virus had one potentially important "weak link" in its life cycle. During the process of replication, the virus produces a very long polypeptide chain made of thousands of amino acids. This chain is similar to a protein except that it is much larger than a typical protein, so it is sometimes called a *superprotein* or a *polyprotein*. It is a polypeptide that contains within itself a number of individual proteins that the virus needs later in its replication. Some of those proteins are used to make the structural components of the cell, while others are used to make the cell's "working parts," nucleic acids and enzymes.

Once the virus makes a polyprotein, it must cut that molecule apart to release all of the individual proteins it needs to continue its replication. The compound it uses to accomplish this task is HIV protease. Proteases are enzymes, a class of compounds that break down other proteins. Researchers realized that the protease step represented a possible point of attack in dealing with HIV. If they could find a way to inactivate the HIV protease, the virus's polyprotein would not be broken down into its component parts, and the components from which new viruses are made would not be available.

The first challenge facing researchers, then, was to determine the precise molecular structure of the HIV protease. That breakthrough occurred in 1989 when a research team at Merck & Company led by Manuel A. Navia reported a structure of the HIV protease molecule, a structure that other research teams later refined. Given that knowledge, drug researchers were able to design molecules with structures compatible with that of the protease molecule that would bond to that molecule and prevent it from carrying out its normal enzymatic operations. The diagram below shows a computer model of the way in which a specially designed compound might combine with the HIV protease molecule and block its action.

Today, about eight new protease-inhibiting drugs have been approved for use by the FDA. All act by bonding in some way or another

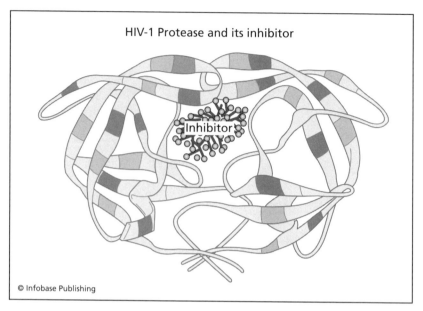

HIV-1 Protease and its inhibitor

Inhibitor

© Infobase Publishing

HIV-1 protease and its inhibitor

with the HIV protease, although the complexity of the protease-drug system is complex enough that each drug uses a different blocking mechanism. The first two antiprotease drugs to be developed were saquinavir (Fortovase®; Invirase®), made by Hoffman-LaRoche and approved for use by the FDA in 1995, and nelfinavir (Viracept®), made by Agouron Pharmaceuticals and approved for use in 1997.

The development of antiprotease drugs like saquinavir and nelfinavir is one of the early triumphs of SAR technology. Knowing the precise molecular structure of protease made it possible for researchers to invent chemical compounds that would fit exactly into the protease structure, bind to the molecule, and prevent it from carrying on the steps needed in the replication of HIV. Drug researchers are hoping that this success will become a model for the development of other drugs. In such cases, they will need to know the chemical structure of enzymes and substrates and the interaction between the two that result in disease. With this knowledge, they may be able to construct new drug molecules that interrupt the disease-causing enzyme-substrate reaction.

Elements of Structure-Activity Relationship Drug Design

In 1909, the great German scientist Paul Ehrlich (1854–1915) suggested a mechanism by which certain molecules exert their pharmacological effects. He said that those molecules contain a region, which he called the *pharmacophore,* specifically responsible for their biological activity. Recall the interaction between enzyme and substrate in the lock-and-key theory of enzyme action. Ehrlich argued that bonding between enzyme and substrate involves only a specific region of the enzyme—the pharmacophore—and understanding the process of bonding requires an understanding specifically of the chemical structure of the pharmacophore, rather than the enzyme as a whole. In 1977, American pharmacologist Peter Gund (1940–) suggested an updated definition for the term *pharmacophore.* He proposed that the term refer to "a set of structural features in a molecule that is recognized at a receptor site and is responsible for that

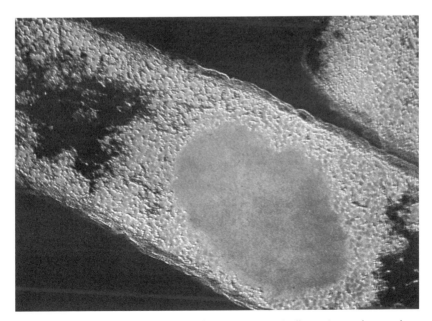

The oval object in this photograph is a bacterium genetically engineered to produce human gamma interferon. (CNRI/Photo Researchers, Inc.)

molecule's biological activity." That is, when a receptor site "sees" an enzyme approaching it, it recognizes a certain characteristic chemical structure—the pharmacophore—to which it can bind. Gund's definition is now widely accepted among chemists.

The concept of a pharmacophore is essential in SAR research because it identifies the specific part of a drug molecule responsible for pharmacological action. It is the part of the molecule, therefore, in which researchers make modifications in their efforts to design new drugs. In studying pharmacophores, chemists focus on three essential properties: (1) the atomic groups present in the pharmacophore; (2) the relative positions of those groups; and (3) the three-dimensional arrangement of the groups when an enzyme bonds to a

Chemical structures of heroin, morphine, and codeine

Some computer programs show the three-dimensional structure of molecules as an aid to designing drugs that can be used against those molecules. (G. Tompkinson/Photo Researchers, Inc.)

substrate. This section deals with methods for finding the structure of a pharmacophore and for making changes in pharmacophore structure in the design of new drugs.

Chemists can deduce the chemical composition of a pharmacophore by comparing the chemical structures of a number of compounds that have similar biological effects and determining what atomic arrangement those compounds have in common. For instance, a number of anesthetics belonging to the morphine family (the opiates) have chemical structures with similar atomic arrangements (see the diagram on page 124). To determine the pharmacophore present in morphine and its analogs, one can remove various groups of atoms from the morphine molecule one at a time to see how the biological potency of the product is affected. Any time the removal of a group diminishes the potency of a compound, one can conclude that the group is essential to the compound's biological activity and, therefore, is part of the molecule's pharmacophore. If the removal of a group has no effect on the compound's biological effects, the group is not part of the molecule's pharmacophore. The diagram shows the atomic grouping found to be the opiate pharmacophore.

Knowledge of a specific pharmacophore allows researchers to design new drugs that may have certain desired effects. For example, researchers at the Wake Forest University School of Medicine and the State University of New York at Buffalo attempted to design drugs that would bind specifically to dopamine receptors in the brains of rats. Dopamine is a neurotransmitter implicated in generation of pleasurable emotions in the brain. Its absence or depletion is thought to be responsible for certain neural disorders, such as psychoses and schizophrenia. Cocaine is believed to bond to dopamine receptors in the brain, resulting in an accumulation of the neurotransmitter and a magnification of its effects on the body. The goal of the research team was to develop cocaine analogs that would bond to dopamine receptors at least as efficiently as does cocaine itself.

Crack cocaine, like that shown here, is made by adding ammonium hydroxide to cocaine hydrochloride, the form in which the drug is most often available. (TEK Image/Photo Researchers, Inc.)

Researchers identified a cocaine pharmacophore thought to bind selectively to dopamine receptors, then synthesized a number of cocaine analogs that also contained that pharmacophore. In 2000, they reported their discovery that these analogs had biological effects similar, to a greater or lesser degree, to those of cocaine. Clearly, these analogs hold the potential for development as drugs that can modify the concentration of dopamine in the brain and, hence, its influence on the senses.

Modifications in Pharmacophores

Any number of changes in the physical or chemical structure of a lead compound can modify its biological activity. These changes tend to fall into one of two general categories: (1) changing the size and shape of the lead compound molecule, or (2) introducing new substituents into the lead compound molecule. Following are some examples of pharmacophore modifications that have been made by researchers and the biological consequences of those changes.

CHANGING SIZE AND SHAPE

A well-studied example of pharmacophore modification by changing size and shape involves the insertion of methylene ($-CH_2-$) groups into the molecular structure of a lead compound. The addition of methylene groups increases the size and alters the shape of a lead compound. Research in this area suggests that the analogs produced in this way differ significantly in their biological potency depending on the number of methylene groups added to the molecule. An example of this research is a classic study carried out by A. R. L. Dohme and his colleagues in the 1920s on a family of compounds known as 4-alkyl resorcinols. These compounds are made by introducing one or more methylene groups at the number 4 position in the resorcinol molecule, as shown in the structural formula on the graph below. As the graph shows, Dohme's group found that the biological potency of the members of this family increased from zero (with one or two methylene groups) to a maximum level (with six methylene groups) and then dropped back to zero with the addition of eight or more methylene groups.

The relationship between added methylene groups and potency depends to some extent on the compound being tested. In a 2000 study on a family of compounds known as the N,N'-diarylalkane-diamides, a team of Czech and Slovak researchers found that increasing the number of methylene groups in a compound from two to seven resulted in a nearly linear increase in the potency of the analog produced. Researchers explained their results by pointing out that methylene groups are nonpolar and tend to increase the tendency of a compound to dissolve in fatty substances, such as those

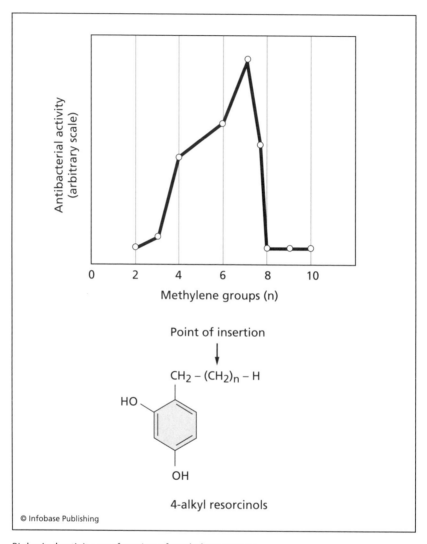

Biological activity as a function of methylene groups

found in the membrane of cells. A moderate increase in the number of methylene groups, then, may improve the ability of a compound to pass through a cell membrane and enter the cell, increasing the likelihood of its being able to act on the cell.

The addition of one or more rings to a lead compound also changes its size and shape. Rings are groups of atoms connected in a circle.

Replacing a hydrogen atom, a methyl group, a hydroxyl, or similar small group by a ring increases the bulk of the lead molecule. The biological potency of such analogs usually cannot be predicted in advance. As an example, the lead compound benzylpenicillin is metabolized by the enzyme β-lactamase. The addition of a ring to benzylpenicillin results in the formation of diphenicillin, which is *not* metabolized by the same enzyme, but the addition of the same ring to benzylpenicillin in a different location on the molecule results in the formation of 2-phenylbenzylpenicillin, which *is* metabolized by β-lactamase. Scientists hypothesize that the addition of the ring in diphenicillin accounts for its resistance to β-lactamase, while the same addition in 2-phenylbenzylpenicillin has an opposite effect because of its different location in the molecule.

Another method for changing the size and shape of a lead compound molecule is by increasing or decreasing the saturation in a molecule, that is, by increasing or decreasing the number of double and triple bonds. Two atoms joined by a double or triple bond are held in a fixed position by the electrons that make up those bonds. By contrast, two atoms joined by a single bond rotate freely around that bond. As an example, consider the simple alkyl halide 1,2-dichloroethane, CH_2ClCH_2Cl. The two carbon atoms in the molecule are free to rotate around the single bond that joins them. Only one form of the molecule exists.

By contrast, consider the unsaturated form of this compound, 1,2-dichloroethene, $CHCl=CHCl$. In this compound, the two carbon atoms are joined by a double bond. The two carbon atoms are held rigidly in position by the double bond and are not able to rotate around each other. Two forms (isomers) of the compound exist. In one isomer, both chlorine atoms are on one side of the double bond (above or below it); in the other isomer, the two chlorine atoms are on opposite sides of the two double (one above and one below). The first isomer is called *cis*-1,2-dichloroethene, and the second, *trans*-1,2-dichloroethene. The way in which each of these two isomers might bond with a receptor site could be very different, resulting in different biological potencies for each compound.

One example of this kind of change in previous research involves the compound cortisol (hydrocortisone), a hormone produced by the adrenal cortex in response to stress. It increases blood pressure and blood sugar levels and suppresses the immune system. The insertion of a double bond in the cortisol molecule results in the formation of a related steroidal hormone known as *prednisone*. Although this change may seem relatively minor, it has a profound effect, resulting in a product whose biological potency is about 30 times that of the parent compound.

Similar results were obtained in a 2001 study on the antiprogesterone drug mifepristone (also known as RU-486 or Mifeprex®). Shifting the location of a double bond by a single carbon atom converted an analog with a high binding affinity for progestin to one that had essentially no binding affinity for the hormone. That is, the position of the double bond in a relatively complex molecule determined the ability of the molecule to act as an antiprogesterone drug.

INTRODUCING NEW SUBSTITUENTS

A second common SAR method used to produce analogs of lead drugs is to introduce a variety of substituents into the lead molecule. Some substituents commonly used in such experiments are alkyl groups, such as methyl (CH_3-), ethyl (C_2H_5-), or propyl (C_3H_7-) groups; halogens (F, Cl, Br, or I); hydroxy (-OH) groups; amino (-NH_2) groups; carboxylic (-COO) groups; and a variety of sulfur-containing groups, such as thiols, sulfides, and sulfonic acid groups. Although the addition of such groups to a parent molecule may change its size and shape, it may also change its chemical and physical properties. For example, such groups may alter the molecule's affinity for water, organic substances, charged regions, and other chemical features of a target molecule. In such a case, an analog produced by adding a substituent to a lead molecule may react with a substrate in an entirely different way from that of the parent molecule, resulting in a totally different biological potency.

One example of the effect of substitution on biological potency involves the popular drug acetaminophen (Tylenol®). Acetaminophen is almost completely metabolized in the liver with the production of harmless products that are excreted through the kidneys. A small amount of the drug may be metabolized, however, to a toxic product, N-acetyl-p-benzo-quinone imine. In cases where large quantities of acetaminophen are ingested, the quantity of N-acetyl-p-benzo-quinone imine produced may be significant, and toxic reactions may occur. Acetaminophen poisoning has become a serious problem in the United States and other parts of the world. In this country, it is now the single most common cause of liver failure, resulting in 74 deaths in 2003.

Researchers have found that the substitution of two methyl groups on the benzene ring in the acetaminophen molecule results in the formation of an analog that is essentially resistant to the metabolic reactions that result in the formation of N-acetyl-p-benzo-quinone imine and, hence, prevent toxic reactions involved with the use of acetaminophen. Researchers believe that the presence of the methyl groups interferes with enzyme actions that, in the first step of the reaction by which N-acetyl-p-benzo-quinone imine is produced, convert hydrogen atoms on the benzene rings in acetaminophen to hydroxyl groups.

Quantitative Structure-Activity Relationships

Structure-activity relationship research has been enormously successful in identifying many kinds of drugs for further development. This approach to rational drug design has one inherent drawback, however: It is difficult to predict the effectiveness of any particular approach to analog design. It is not uncommon for a researcher to design an experiment for the preparation of a half dozen analogs of a known antibiotic, with the hope that all or some of them will have useful biological activity, only to discover that *none* of the compounds is biologically active.

One way of dealing with this drawback is a modification of SAR research known as quantitative structure-activity relationships (QSAR). In QSAR, researchers attempt to use quantitative techniques for describing a variety of physical and chemical properties. For example, hydrogen bonds tend to form between hydrogen atoms and centers of negative charge, and that information can be useful in designing drug analogs to react with certain kinds of target receptor cells, enzymes, or other biological objects. The design process can be much more efficient if the process of

◁ **LOUIS PLACK HAMMETT (1894–1987)** ▷

Organic chemistry, as its name suggests, originally grew out of a somewhat different history than did inorganic chemistry. For many years, chemists tended to assume that organic compounds—defined at the time as compounds that are part of or produced by living organisms—were somehow fundamentally different from inorganic compounds, compounds associated only with rocks, stones, minerals, and other types of nonliving materials. In fact, organic compounds were for many decades thought to contain some "living principle" that made them resistant to synthesis by "mere" human chemists.

The growth of modern organic chemistry as a science is, to a large extent, dependent on chemists' recognition that organic compounds are fundamentally the same as inorganic compounds, often much larger and more complex, but subject, nonetheless, to the same laws of physics that control the behavior of all atoms and molecules. An important contributor to that understanding was Louis Plack Hammett who, during the 1920s, studied the quantitative physical properties of many different organic compounds. Among his many accomplishments was the derivation of an equation still widely used in organic chemistry, particularly in the field of quantitative structure-activity relationships (QSAR), the so-called Hammett equation. That equation, commonly written as $\log(k_s/k_0) = \rho\sigma$, where k_s and k_0 are the ionization constants for a substituted benzene product and for benzene itself and ρ and σ are two constants related to the aromatic compounds under investigation. The great value of the Hammett equation is that it has been found to have applications that extend far beyond the somewhat narrow process that Hammett originally investigated and therefore provides a powerful tool in the general procedures used in QSAR.

Louis Plack Hammett was born in Wilmington, Delaware, on April 7, 1894, while his parents were visiting from their native New England. Hammett grew up in Portland, Maine, where he fell in love with chemistry during his high school years. After graduation, he enrolled at Harvard College, his father's alma mater, where he majored in physical and organic chemistry. Hammett was awarded his A.B. degree from Harvard in 1916 and also received a

hydrogen bond formation can be expressed mathematically, with an equation that expresses the precise amount of attraction between two chemical entities.

Sheldon Traveling Scholarship that allowed him to spend a year studying with the great German chemist and Nobel Prize winner Hermann Staudinger (1881–1965). He returned to the United States in 1917 fully expecting to be drafted into the U.S. Army. Instead, he was assigned to do research on paints and varnishes used on airplane bodies. After the war, he spent about a year working in industry before enrolling at Columbia University for his doctoral studies. He was awarded his Ph.D. in organic chemistry by Columbia in 1923. He was then offered a job in the chemistry department at Columbia, a position he held for the rest of his academic career.

It was at Columbia that Hammett carried out his research on the physical properties of organic compounds that made him famous. His first accomplishment was his development of a concept now known as the *acidity function*, a new interpretation of the behavior of acids in concentrated and dilute solutions. He also derived the Hammett equation and Hammett function for organic substances, accomplishments for which he is perhaps best known today. In 1940, he published his textbook *Physical-Organic Chemistry*, which some chemists have called "one of the great textbooks in the history of chemistry."

With the onset of World War II, Hammett took a leave of absence from Columbia to become first associate director and later director of the National Defense Research Committee's Explosives Research Laboratory in Bruceton, Pennsylvania, just outside Pittsburgh. During his tenure, the laboratory made a number of important inventions that contributed to the success of the war effort. After the war, Hammett returned to Columbia, where he remained until his retirement in 1961. He spent the last 25 years of his life in the Quaker retirement community of Medford Leas, New Jersey, where he died on February 9, 1987.

During his lifetime, Hammett was awarded the Priestley Medal of the American Chemical Society (1961) and the National Medal of Science (1967). In 1997, he was selected by readers of the chemical journal *Chemical & Engineering News* as one of the 75 most distinguished contributors to the field of science in the preceding 75 years. He served as chairman of the National Research Council's chemistry and chemical technology division from 1946 to 1947 and was chair of the board of the American Chemical Society for 1961.

Credit for the earliest proposals for expressing a mathematical connection between chemical and physical properties and biological effects is usually given to a pair of Scottish physicians, Alexander

Crum Brown (1838–1922) and T. R. Fraser. In 1868, Crum Brown and Fraser suggested that the physiological actions produced by a substance could be expressed mathematically as a function of the substance's chemical constitution, or $\Phi = f(C)$. They failed to develop any specific example of this principle and, indeed, the subject of QSAR remained largely dormant until the 1930s. Then, the American chemist Louis Plack Hammett (1894–1987) was able to develop a number of mathematical relationships relating the physical and chemical characteristics of a compound to its biological activity. The *Hammett constant* and *Hammett equation* are still essential parts of QSAR-based drug design today.

In fact, QSAR has now become one of the most powerful tools of rational drug design, an approach that is used in the development of a host of new products in pharmacy and other fields of biological research.

Combinatorial Chemistry

For all the progress SAR and QSAR have brought to drug development programs, they still have some fundamental flaws. Perhaps the most important, from a commercial standpoint, is that they are slow and expensive ways of developing new drugs. In an effort to overcome these flaws, researchers are constantly looking for new ways to design and produce novel drugs. One of the most successful alternative methods involves a revolutionary new process known as combinatorial chemistry, sometimes abbreviated as combichem.

Combinatorial chemistry can truly be called revolutionary because it is based on a model of chemical synthesis that is totally different from that traditionally used for the synthesis of new chemical compounds. As every high school student of chemistry knows, the conventional method for making a chemical compound, AB, is by combining its two components, A and B, as represented in the equation:

$$A + B \rightarrow AB$$

Other modes of synthesis are, of course, possible. For example, a double replacement reaction may be used to make AB from two compounds rather than from two elements:

$$AX + YB \rightarrow AB + YX$$

In all such cases, however, the product can be obtained by reacting no more than two or three reactants.

In inorganic chemistry, the product AB is often produced in a relatively pure form, with few by-products from which it must be separated. In organic chemistry, the field in which drug research is carried out, AB tends to be only one of many products formed. A more accurate representation of the synthesis of AB in organic chemistry is represented by the following equation:

$$A + B \rightarrow AB + w + x + y + z + \ldots,$$

where w, x, y, and z are by-products from which the desired product, AB, must be separated.

Combinatorial chemistry, by contrast, involves the reaction of one *set* of compounds with a second *set* of compounds, each set belonging to a particular family of compounds. For example, one set of compounds might consist of primary alcohols, and the second set, of carboxylic acids. The products of the reactions between these two sets of compounds would, then, be a set of all esters (the compounds formed when carboxylic acids react with alcohols) that could be synthesized from the alcohols and acids in each group.

The members of one set of compounds can be represented with the symbol A_x and the members of the second set with the symbol B_y. Then the reactions that occur between the two sets of compounds can be represented as

$$A_x + B_y \rightarrow A_r B_s,$$

where $A_r B_s$ represents all possible compounds that can be produced by the reaction of all the members of the first set of compounds with all of the members of the second set. The range of all possible such reactions can be diagrammed as shown below, with the crossed lines representing the reaction between each member of the A set with each member of the B set.

The number of unique products produced in a reaction of this kind is equal to the product of the number of reactants in each set. If there are 10 members of the A set, for example, and 20 members

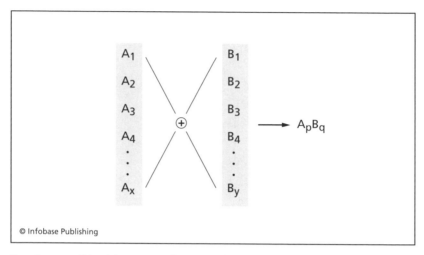

© Infobase Publishing

Reactions possible with two sets of compounds, A and B

of the B set, then 200 (10 × 20) unique products are obtained from the reaction. The complete set of all products in such a reaction is called a *library*.

The great advantage of this approach to synthesis is, of course, speed. Making the 200 compounds in the library just discussed by traditional methods would take a very long time, considerable money, and much labor. In fact, costs and time constraints would probably make the process prohibitive by traditional techniques. In combinatorial chemistry, however, the 200 compounds in the library can be made all at once with relatively little cost and expenditure of time and money. The only problem (and a significant problem it is!) is to find out which of the 200 compounds (if any) meet some predetermined criterion, such as biological potency.

Two general methods are used to build a library of compounds by the general techniques of combinatorial chemistry: *solid-phase synthesis* (SPS) and *solution-phase synthesis*.

Solid-Phase Synthesis

The general principles on which solid-phase synthesis is based were elucidated in a 1963 paper by Bruce Merrifield (1921–2006), who was awarded the Nobel Prize in chemistry in 1984 for his work. Merrifield's work involved the synthesis of peptides, large molecules that consist of many amino acids joined to each other in a linear chain. His methodology has since been extended to a number of other areas, perhaps most significantly the design and development of new drugs. A number of modifications have also been developed in the procedure originally invented by Merrifield. Nonetheless, understanding his procedure is essential to understanding the fundamental principles of combinatorial chemistry.

The Merrifield method of peptide synthesis is deceptively simple. As shown in the diagram below, it begins with some means of solid support for the synthesis, *resin beads* in Merrifield's original work, to which is attached a single molecule that can serve as the basis (the monomer) for a far more complex molecule. In Merrifield's original research, the molecule attached to the resin bead was an amino acid molecule.

Next, the resin bead–amino acid complex is washed with a solution of a second type of molecule, another amino acid in Merrifield's

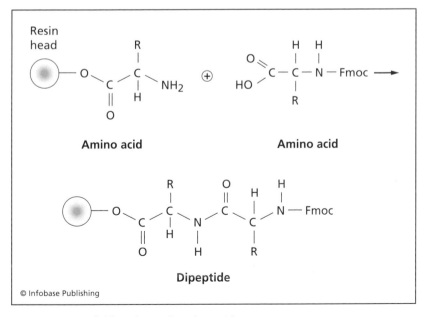

First step in Merrifield synthesis of a polypeptide

approach. The second amino acid is modified ("protected") to prevent it from reacting with other substances present in the reaction chamber. The two most common protecting groups are *tert*-butyloxycarbonyl (Boc) and fluorenylmethoxycarbonyl (Fmoc). (Today,

◁ R. BRUCE MERRIFIELD (1921–2006) ▷

An American biochemist, Robert Bruce Merrifield conducted research that revolutionized the way chemical synthesis is done in a variety of fields, including drug development.

Merrifield was born in Fort Worth, Texas, on July 15, 1921. He was the only son of George E. and Lorene (Lucas) Merrifield. When Bruce (as he was generally known) was only two years old, his family left Fort Worth for California, and they moved frequently thereafter. Young Bruce attended nine elementary schools and two high schools, eventually graduating from Montebello High School in 1939. Merrifield enrolled at Pasadena Junior College and received his associate's degree in 1941. He then transferred to the University of California at Los Angeles (UCLA), where he was awarded his bachelor's degree in chemistry in 1943. Merrifield then spent a year working as a chemist at the Philip R. Park Research Foundation, where he was in charge of experimental animals used in research. After only a year at the Park Foundation, Merrifield realized that he needed further education if he were to advance beyond his animal-care job. So he returned to UCLA to begin graduate studies in biochemistry. Over the next five years, Merrifield was a teaching assistant in the chemistry department and a research assistant at the UCLA School of Medicine while he studied for his degree. In 1949, he was awarded his Ph.D. at UCLA, and a day after graduation he left for New York City and his new job as a research assistant at the Rockefeller Institute for Medical Research, later renamed Rockefeller University.

Over the next two decades, Merrifield worked his way up the academic ladder at Rockefeller. He was appointed assistant professor in 1957, associate professor in 1958, and full professor in 1966. In 1983, he was promoted again, this time to the position of John D. Rockefeller Jr. Professor of the Rockefeller University. In 1968, Merrifield also served as Nobel Guest Professor at Uppsala University in Sweden.

During his early years at Rockefeller, Merrifield worked in the laboratory of the eminent biochemist D. W. Woolley (1914–66) who, at the time, was

protected amino acids containing either Boc or Fmoc are commercially available so that researchers do not have to go through the
additional step of making their own protected compounds for use
in an SPS synthesis.) The product of this reaction now contains two

interested in peptide and nucleotide growth factors. This research required
the synthesis of peptides and led to Merrifield's discovery of the principles of solid-phase synthesis, for which he was awarded the Nobel Prize.
Although Merrifield had established the major elements of that procedure
by the early 1960s, the scientific community did not recognize its possibilities until more than two decades later. Today, Merrifield's method is generally acknowledged as one of the great technical breakthroughs in peptide
research in the history of the science. It provides a relatively simple, rapid,
and dependable method for the synthesis of peptides, proteins, nucleic
acids, and other large molecules, an essential step in drug development,
gene technology, and other fields. Procedures that once required months
or years to complete are now accomplished in a matter of hours with the
Merrifield technique.

In addition to the Nobel Prize, Merrifield received numerous other awards,
including the Lasker Award for Basic Medical Research (1969), the Gairdner
Award for outstanding biomedical research (1970), the American Chemical
Society (ACS) Award for Creative Work in Synthetic Organic Chemistry (1972),
the Nichols Medal of the New York Chapter of the ACS (1973), the American
Peptide Society's Alan E. Pierce Award (1979), the Science Award from Big
Brothers, Inc. of New York City (1988), the Royal Society of Chemistry Medal
(1987), the Ralph F. Hirschmann Award from the ACS (1990), and the Glenn T.
Seaborg Medal presented by the UCLA Department of Chemistry and
Biochemistry (1993).

Merrifield retired from Rockefeller University in 1992 with the title of
Professor Emeritus. He then accepted a research position as adjunct professor at the Oregon Institute of Science and Medicine in Cave Junction,
Oregon. The Institute calls itself "a small research institute" devoted to the
study of "biochemistry, diagnostic medicine, nutrition, preventive medicine
and the molecular biology of aging." It consists of six faculty members,
including its founder, Arthur B. Robinson, a one-time colleague of Linus
Pauling. Merrifield died after a long illness at Cresskill, New Jersey, on May
14, 2006.

units joined to each other and attached to the solid support. In the Merrifield procedure, the product is a dipeptide, a two-unit amino acid, attached to a resin bead. The protecting group (the Boc or Fmoc group) must then be removed from the amino acid just added so that it can react with a third unit to be added.

The procedure described above can now be repeated. First the reaction chamber is washed with a solution containing the third unit to be added (the third amino acid). This amino acid is also protected with either a Boc or Fmoc protective group. When the third unit is added to the existing two-unit structure, a three-unit (tripeptide) product is obtained. The protecting group is then removed and a fourth group added to permit the process to continue. The process can then be repeated as often as desired.

The Merrifield method has a number of attractive characteristics beyond the simple steps outlined here. For example, because the product molecule (such as the monomer, dimer, or trimer) is attached to a solid support, a chemist can apply other operations to the system without fear of losing that product. The reaction system can be washed at almost any point. This property is very useful, for example, because it allows the chemist to remove excess reactant or undesired by-products of the reaction.

Most important of all, however, is the possibility of running the Merrifield procedure on any number of resin beads (or other support systems) simultaneously in a number of reaction chambers. An example of this alternative is the so-called *split and mix system* of combinatorial chemistry. The first step in this kind of system is to prepare some number of monomer-support units (three in the example shown below), in which the monomer present differs from chamber to chamber. In the diagram below, the units are represented as •-X, •-Y, and •-Z. These three units are washed and then mixed with each other in a single container. The mixture is then divided and placed into three separate containers. One of the most common containers used contains a number of wells in a plastic or glass dish that are miniature versions of the common petri dish used in biology experiments.

The three wells now contain all three of the monomer-support units, •-X, •-Y, and •-Z. In the next step, monomer X is added to the first well, monomer Y to the second well, and monomer Z to the

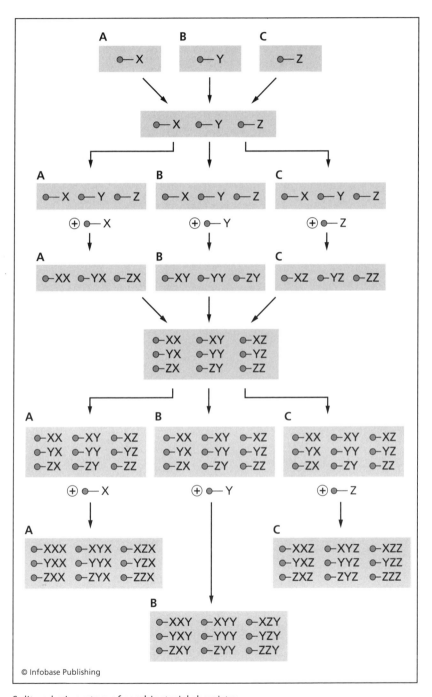

Split and mix system of combinatorial chemistry

third well. The products of these reactions are the dimers •-X-X, •-Y-X, and •-Z-X in the first well, •-X-Y, •-Y-Y, and •-Z-Y in the second well, and •-X-Z, •-Y-Z, and •-Z-Z in the third well.

Again, the components of the three wells are mixed and then split into three separate chambers. Each of the three wells now contains all possible dimers of the three monomers, •-X-X, •-X-Y, •-X-Z, •-Y-X, •-Y-Y, •-Y-Z, •-Z-X, •-Z-Y, and •-Z-Z. Once more, the three monomers are added to each of the three wells, X to the first well, Y to the second well, and Z to the third well. The products of these reactions consist of the 27 possible trimers that can be made with the three monomers arranged in all possible combinations.

This example is a greatly simplified version of the type of syntheses that are usually carried out in combinatorial chemistry because only three monomers are used and only three steps are shown. If this process were continued for only three more steps, the number of products (hexamers) possible would be 729. If the number of different monomers used were five rather than three, the number of trimers possible would be 125 (rather than 27 in this example) and the number of hexamers, 15,625. Not uncommonly, a researcher might use 10 different monomers in an experiment, permitting the formation of 1,000 different trimers or a million (10^6) hexamers. A person working in the field of peptide chemistry, with the 20 naturally occurring amino acids for use as monomers, could synthesize 8,000 trimers or 64 million hexamers. Calculating the number of proteinlike molecules (peptides containing a few hundred or a few thousand amino acid monomers) yields a very large number indeed. The number of moderate-sized proteins, for example, has been estimated at about 20^{124}.

A key element in the original Merrifield procedure of solid-phase synthesis is the solid support system. That system consists of two parts: a resin bead and a *linker,* an organic compound used to join the first amino acid to the resin bead. The resin beads used by Merrifield are small spherical objects made of cross-linked polystyrene. This material consists primarily of the polymer polystyrene whose linear molecules are linked to each other at various positions by the addition of divinylbenzene ($CH_2 = CHC_6H_4CH = CH_2$). The final cross-linked material is relatively rigid, with enough flexibility to permit swelling when it is placed in liquid. It is also inert to most reagents used in SPS procedures. It is generally prepared in the form of small spherical beads with diameters of about 80 to 200 μm.

The linker in a support system has two functions: first, to provide an anchor for the growing polymer being made during the synthesis, and second, to protect the functional group at one end of that polymer, the end attached to the resin. At the completion of the synthesis, the final product is released from the linker, which remains attached to the resin bead.

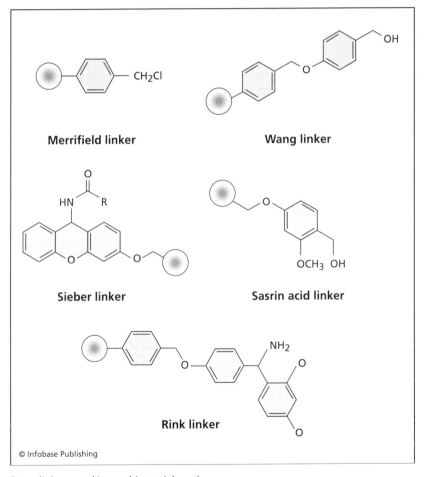

Some linkers used in combinatorial syntheses

A variety of functional groups have been used as linkers. Each type of linker has its advantages and disadvantages, depending on the type of polymer being made and the conditions under which synthesis occurs. In his earliest work, Merrifield employed a chlorinated benzene group. The chlorine in this functional group provides an active site that can react with the monomer that is to be added to it. A popular alternative linker that has been developed is the so-called Wang linker, also known as the hydroxymethylphenoxy (HMP) linker. In this case, the hydroxy group at the end of the linker is the active site at which addition of the monomer takes place. These and a number of other linkers used in various types of synthesis reactions are shown in the diagram on page 143.

Like almost any other type of technology, resin beads have certain technical drawbacks, one of which is their tendency to induce a growing peptide chain to begin folding into a three-dimensional shape, reducing access to the functional group at the end of the chain. To overcome this and other disadvantages, a number of other solid support systems have been designed. One system that has gained considerable popularity among researchers is the TentaGel™ resin, produced by the German chemical firm of Rapp Polymere. These resins are made of a cross-linked polystyrene matrix onto which is grafted a layer of polyethylene glycol. Rapp Polymere describes the material as a "chameleon type" polymer since it can exhibit both hydrophobic and hydrophilic properties, making it suitable for a wide variety of reaction conditions in combinatorial experiments. Rapp Polymere now offers at least a half dozen different varieties of TentaGel™, each with structural adaptations that make it especially suitable for specific types of SPS experiments.

Many other solid support systems have also been devised for dealing with the problems presented by traditional resin beads and other technical issues. One such issue, discussed later in this section, involves the identification of specific compounds within a library that have desired biological effects. One of the earliest of these alternative support systems was invented in 1984 by Richard Houghten, then a researcher at the Scripps Research Institute in La Jolla, California. In searching for a way to speed up the synthesis of peptides by the Merrifield method, Houghten suggested using small

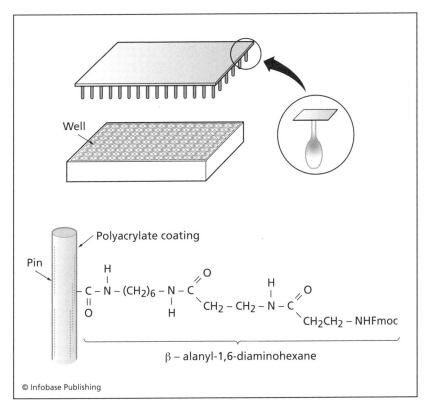

Multipin system used in solid phase synthesis

mesh bags made of the polymer polypropylene to hold batches of resin beads. These bags were roughly 15 by 20 mm in size with pores of about 75 μm in diameter, too small to permit escape of the beads from the bag, but large enough to permit diffusion of solvent and solutes used in the synthesis of peptides. Houghten later explained that the term *tea bags* for these small containers was inspired by a colleague's having pinned an actual tea bag to a poster describing his work at a conference where he was making a presentation.

Another system proposed for use in solid-phase systems is called the *multipin system,* originally developed by H. Mario Geysen, then at Australia's Commonwealth Serum Laboratories. Geysen's system makes use of one of the most popular tools of immunological research, the 96-well polyethylene plate consisting of eight rows of 12 wells each into which samples are deposited. The multipin system is named for a set of 96 polyethylene pins attached to a polyethylene plate placed in position to correspond exactly with the 96 wells on the traditional immunological analysis plate. The diagram on page 145 shows the structure of a multipin system.

Each pin in the system is 40 mm in length and 4 mm in diameter. The pins are made of polyethylene, which is treated with high-energy gamma radiation in a 6 percent aqueous solution of acrylic acid ($H_2C = CHCOOH$). This treatment converts the acrylic acid to polyacrylate, which forms a thin surface on top of the polyethylene pins. A molecule of a β-alanyl-1,6-diaminohexane is then attached to the pin and deactivated with a Fmoc protective group. This arrangement is shown at the bottom of the multipin diagram above.

The stage is then set for a solid-phase synthesis. The monomer to be used in the synthesis is added to the 96 wells in the polyethylene plate. The protecting Fmoc groups are removed from the ends of the pins, and the pins themselves are inserted into the 96 wells. At this point, the monomer in each well reacts with the exposed carboxylate group on the end of the pin, producing the monomer-support complex (comparable to that present in the first step of resin-bead-based SPS). The 96-pin plate is then removed from the 96-well plate, and the pins are washed and reinserted into a second 96-well plate that contains the second monomer to be added. The 96-pin plate is removed, washed again, and reinserted into a third 96-well plate for the addition of a third monomer. The process is repeated as often as necessary to produce the polymers to be produced in the synthesis.

The discussion so far has described how libraries of potentially active chemical compounds can be produced using solid-phase synthesis. The next question—and a crucial question it is—is which of those compounds meet the basic criteria for which the experiment was intended? One might ask, for example, which compounds of all those in the library are actually potent in the treatment of some disease. The process by which the structure of any active compound present in a mixture of compounds is identified is called *deconvolution*. Deconvolution is often one of the most time-consuming steps in any combinatorial procedure.

Recall the example discussed earlier in which 27 different compounds were generated in an SPS experiment. How is one to decide which of those 27 compounds, if any, is biologically active? One approach is the following.

First, one tests the biological activity of each of the three containers, A, B, and C. For example, one might add a drop taken from each container to a petri dish containing the organism against which action is desired. Assume that only the liquid from container A shows any biological activity, that is, kills the organism on the petri dish. This result reveals the first piece of information needed to determine the structure of the active compound present in the library: All of the compounds in container A have an X as their final unit.

The next step involves going back one step in the synthesis process, in this case to the dimer level. The monomer X is now added to each container, resulting in the formation of three new sets of trimers with the structures shown below.

CONTAINER D	CONTAINER E	CONTAINER F
X-X-X	X-Y-X	X-Z-X
Y-X-X	Y-Y-X	Y-Z-X
Z-X-X	Z-Y-X	Z-Z-X

Notice that the nine possible compounds originally in container A are now divided into three distinct new containers, D, E, and F. The contents of each of these containers are now tested for biological activity.

Assume that of the three, only container F shows biological activity. This result shows that the second-to-last monomer in the compound must be a Z. One now has two of the three components of the final product. The third component at this point can be determined rather easily by a straightforward chemical analysis.

Of course, identifying the biological potency of more complex compounds is far more difficult than the process shown here, but the principle is essentially the same: a process of iteration, repeated testing by which one compound after another of the active compound is determined.

The value of synthesizing libraries of useful compounds by a variety of SPS techniques is unquestionable. However, SPS does have some significant drawbacks. One is that not all possible synthetic reactions that a researcher one might want to study can be carried out with SPS. Another is that it may take a significant amount of time and effort to develop an SPS procedure through which a particular product can be obtained. Finally, measuring the progress of a reaction and the purity of intermediate products can also be a challenge. In many situations, in fact, a more traditional approach to synthesis using an all-liquid environment may be preferable to SPS. An important advantage of this approach, known as *solution-phase synthesis,* is that the chemistry of such reactions is generally well known, having been a part of the basic paradigm of most chemical research for well over a century. It is also the method most familiar to high-school chemistry students. The primary challenge with solution-phase synthesis, on the other hand, is to separate and purify products of the reaction such that the one or more compounds with biological potency (or some other desirable feature) can be collected and identified.

Solution-Phase Synthesis

Although it uses an all-liquid environment, like traditional procedures, the methods of solution-phase synthesis (also called *parallel synthesis* or *multiple parallel synthesis*) are distinct. The difference is illustrated below.

Traditional methods:

$$A + B \rightarrow AB$$

followed by:

$$AB + C \rightarrow ABC$$

Parallel synthesis:

$$+ B_1 \rightarrow AB_1$$

$$+ B_2 \rightarrow AB_2$$

$$A \qquad + B_3 \rightarrow AB_3$$

$$+ B_4 \rightarrow AB_4 \ldots$$

$$+ B_n \rightarrow AB_n$$

Followed by:

$$+ AB_1 \rightarrow AB_1C$$

$$+ AB_2 \rightarrow AB_2C$$

$$C \qquad + AB_3 \rightarrow AB_3C$$

$$+ AB_4 \rightarrow AB_4C \ldots$$

$$+ AB_n \rightarrow AB_nC$$

Repeated as many times as desired.

Parallel synthesis obviously allows the preparation of many more compounds at once than is possible with traditional techniques. The number of possible compounds that can be generated by this method can be increased by using *two families* of reactants, rather than a single family and a single compound.

Imagine a simplified example in which six different primary alcohols (R_1OH through R_6OH) are combined with six different carboxylic acids (R_7COOH through $R_{12}COOH$). In this situation, each alcohol reacts with all six carboxylic acids, producing six esters, and, conversely, each carboxylic acid reacts with all six alcohols, also producing six esters. In all, 36 different esters can be produced simultaneously by the procedure.

Most practical cases of parallel synthesis are, of course, considerably more complex than this example. For instance, in 2004, researchers at the University of Cologne in Germany and the Chemspeed Company reported on their efforts to obtain a better understanding of the way in which cell receptors work. They synthesized a library of 24 forms of a compound called 2-(guanidiniocarbonyl)-1H-pyrroles, known to bind to carboxylates at cell surfaces. They produced these 24 compounds by reacting the guanidinocarbonyl-pyrrole-carboxylate ion with a variety of primary amines. Significantly, the researchers used automated equipment that allowed them to produce the complete library within a 24-hour period. They found that all 24 of the compounds bonded to inorganic species commonly involved in cell receptor reactions.

As in solid-phase synthesis programs, one of the most challenging problems with solution-phase synthesis is to separate products obtained in the reaction mixtures and identify the compound or compounds with biological potency or some other desirable property. An especially effective technique that has been developed to deal with this problem is called *indexed libraries,* also known as *orthogonal libraries.* In this process, each product compound is prepared twice. Analysis then permits identification of the positive part of the compound and the negative part of the compound with the greatest potency. Once these have been determined, it is possible to identify the specific compound most active in the mixture.

Suppose, for example, that one wishes to prepare all possible compounds produced in the reaction between a group of related compounds, A, and a second group of related compounds, B. (The first set of compounds might, for example, be a group of primary amines and the second set, a group of alkyl halides.) In this case, the reaction that occurs can be represented by the general equation:

$$RNH_2 + R'X \rightarrow RR'NH + HX$$

The members of each group could be represented as A_1, A_2, A_3, A_4 ... A_n, and the members of the second group as B_1, B_2, B_3, B_4 ... B_n. The first set of compounds is synthesized by allowing the first member of set A (A_1) to react with each of the members of the B set. The next set is produced by allowing the second member of the set (A_2) to react with each member of the B set, and so on. The compounds produced as a result of these reactions would have the general form A_1B_1, A_1B_2, A_1B_3, A_1B_4 ...; A_2B_1, A_2B_2, A_2B_3, A_2B_4, and so on. A second set of compounds can then be synthesized by reacting each of the members of the B set with all members of the A set in exactly the same way. The products of these reactions would be of the form B_1A_1, B_1A_2, B_1A_3, B_1A_4 ...; B_2A_1, B_2A_2, B_2A_3, B_2A_4, and so on. A summary of all the compounds produced by this process can be represented in a chart of the following structure:

REACTANTS	A_1	A_2	A_3	A_4
B_1	A_1B_1	A_2B_1	A_3B_1	A_4B_1
B_2	A_1B_2	A_2B_2	A_3B_2	A_4B_2 ←
B_3	A_1B_3	A_2B_3	A_3B_3	A_4B_3
B_4	A_1B_4	A_2B_4	A_3B_4	A_4B_4
		↑		

To determine the one or more compounds in this table that actually meet certain criteria (such as biological potency), one tests each possible mixture: A_1B_n (A_1 combined with each B), A_2B_n (A_2 combined with each B) . . . B_1A_n (B_1 with each A), B_2A_n (B_2 with each A), and so on. Suppose the result of that test is that the two mixtures indicated with arrows in the chart above (row 2 and column 3) show the greatest degree of activity. In that case, the most potent compound produced in the total set of all reactions must be A_3B_2.

Orthogonal testing tends to work most successfully with relatively small libraries, like the one described here. The larger the number of compounds being synthesized, the more mixtures have to be tested. This problem has not proved to be insurmountable, however. In the first report on orthogonal testing, for example, published in 1994 by a research team at Glaxo Research and Development in Middlesex, United Kingdom, the method was used to analyze a total of 1,600 amides and esters produced in the reactions among 40 acid chlorides and 40 amine and alcohol nucleophiles. Other studies have been even more ambitious. Richard Houghten and C. T. Dooley have reported, for example, that they used orthogonal screening to analyze a library of 34 million (18^6)

hexapeptides obtained from six sets of mixtures, each mixture containing 1,889,568 (18^5) compounds.

The process of orthogonal testing highlights one of the major technical challenges in solution-phase processes: the separation of individual products from each other. In SPS, of course, products are, by definition, always attached to some kind of solid support, such as resin beads or pins. In solution-phase experiments, products are thoroughly mixed with each other. Even if one can identify which among all possible products are desirable, some way must be found to separate those products from those of no interest to the experimenter and from excess reagents that may be present in the reaction mixture.

One method that has been developed to deal with this challenge is called *fluorous synthesis,* or *fluorous solution chemistry.* The principles of fluorous chemistry were developed in the late 1990s by University of Pittsburgh chemistry professor Dennis Curran. Curran based his new technique on the fact that fluorous compounds (compounds that contain a number of fluorine atoms) are chemically quite different from both organic and inorganic compounds. That is, if one were to prepare three different solutions—one organic, one inorganic, and one fluorous—and mix all three solutions together, three distinct phases will form; the three solutions are all essentially insoluble in each other.

In a study reported in 2001, Curran described research designed to synthesize a library of analogs of a natural product called mappicine. A ketone derivative of mappicine had been shown to be effective in the treatment of the herpes virus and cytomegalovirus. Curran's research team was interested in determining whether there were analogs of mappicine that also display antiviral action.

The initial reactants in Curran's experiment were a set of seven different pyridinyl alcohols (alcoholic derivatives of pyridine), each "tagged" with a characteristic fluorocarbon grouping. (The "tags" consisted of heavily fluorinated hydrocarbon chains ranging in size from $-C_3F_7$ to $-C_{10}F_{21}$.) The seven tagged pyridinyl alcohols were then mixed together in a single container, and a single monomer was added to the container, bringing about the first series of reactions. The mixture in the container was then divided into eight new containers, and each of the eight was subdivided again into 10 containers, producing a total of 80 separate containers, all of which held the labeled product from the first step. A second addend was then added to each of the 80 containers, producing 80 versions of seven altered forms of the original, or a total of 560 analogs of mappicine. These analogs could be separated from each other because they fell into seven groups, each defined by the fluorocarbon tag added to the pyridinyl alcohols with which the experiment began. Separation of these classes can be accomplished in a variety of ways, such as differential solubility with fluorous solvents or chromatographic separation using fluorous products. Once the analog classes have been separated from each other, the fluorous tags they contain can be removed and the pure products can be isolated for further analysis and testing.

A second method used to separate desired products from excess reactants and by-products formed during the reaction in solution-phase synthesis makes use of so-called *scavenger resins*. Scavenger resins are polymers that have been especially designed to react with excess reactant, by-products, or other species present in a reaction that must be removed in order to obtain a pure product. Scavenger resins can be classified into two general groups: *nucleophiles* and *electrophiles*. A *nucleophile* is an ion or molecule that donates a pair of electrons to some other substance which, in turn, receives those electrons, generally with the formation of a covalent bond. The substance that receives the pair of electrons is called an *electrophile*.

Scavenger resins, like resin beads discussed above, are generally made of polystyrene or some similar polymer that has been cross-linked (chemically combined) with a second polymer, such as divinylbenzene, that gives the polymer some rigidity and allows it to expand when it becomes moist. Because of their size, scavenger resins are capable of holding more than one functional group, allowing them to be used for the scavenging of more than one substance at a time.

To appreciate the way a scavenger resin works, refer again to the simple reaction between a primary amine and an alkyl halide:

$$RNH_2 + R'X \rightarrow RR'NH + HX$$

Assume that in some experiment, an excess of amine has been added to a given quantity of alkyl halide. The task facing a researcher,
then, may be to remove excess amine remaining in the reaction
mixture after the reaction has gone to completion. A scavenger resin
used for this purpose would consist of a polymer base that has been
chemically modified to react with amines. Today, a number of such
resins have been developed and are commercially available. Two
examples of such resins available from the Sigma-Aldrich company
are an activated ketone and a borohydride (see the figure). Sigma-
Aldrich and other companies also offer a variety of other kinds of
scavenger resins for use with amines and a number of other families of compounds.

When added to a reaction mixture, such scavengers react with
excess reactant present in the mixture, forming a complex that is
insoluble because of the resin present in the product. For example,
if the Sigma-Aldrich activated ketone is used as the scavenger with a
primary amine (RNH_2), the reaction that occurs is as follows:

© Infobase Publishing

Examples of scavenger resins

Example of a scavenger reaction

The reactant-scavenger complex can then be removed from the reaction mixture by filtration, leaving behind the desired product in solution in the filtrate, from which it can be removed by standard procedures.

The use of scavenger resins in solution-phase synthesis illustrates a type of procedure that is actually a hybrid between solution-phase and solid-phase methods. The first step of this procedure is clearly a form of solution-phase synthesis since the reactions take place totally within a dissolved state with no solid support provided for any of the reactants. The separation stage of the process occurs only after products have become attached to solid supports—the scavenger resins—from which they may or may not then be removed.

In fact, the distinction between solid-phase and solution-phase processes is largely of historical interest and does not necessarily describe the range of experiments now being carried out in combinatorial chemistry. Researchers are finding ways of using elements from both approaches through which a library of products can be synthesized and then purified and analyzed in the most effective manner possible.

Applications of Combinatorial Chemistry

As indicated earlier in this chapter, combinatorial procedures were originally developed for the purpose of synthesizing peptides, long chains of amino acids. Applications of the technique were immediately obvious in the design and synthesis of other kinds of long-chain molecules, such as nucleic acids, compounds in which many nucleotides are joined to each other to form a polymer. The value of this technology for the development of drugs was also acknowledged soon after Merrifield's method of solid-phase synthesis became widely known.

Today, all pharmaceutical companies are devoting at least some portion of their research budget to the use of combinatorial techniques for the production of new lead compounds for drug development. An early example of this kind of research was a study conducted by scientists at the pharmaceutical firm of Eli Lilly and Company. The study involved an effort to find lead compounds that might be effective in the treatment of migraine, a severe type of headache that affects an estimated 28 million Americans at some time in their lives. Research has shown that the neurotransmitter serotonin may be involved in the onset of migraine. Evidence suggests that compounds with the ability to block certain serotonin receptors in the brain can relieve the symptoms of migraine.

Acting on this basic information, Lilly researchers in the mid-1990s synthesized a library of about 500 analogs of serotonin for testing as possible lead compounds in the treatment of migraine. The research program produced a number of possible lead compounds in a remarkably short time, allowing the first human testing to begin less than two years after the study began. One of the most promising of the lead compounds discovered was named LY334370, a compound that has since been subjected to intensive analysis and testing with both experimental animals and humans. Some observers predict that LY334370 may become one of the first commercially available drugs produced by combinatorial techniques.

Enthusiasm for the use of combinatorial chemistry in the design of new drugs has been offset to some extent by the lack of commercial success for the procedure thus far. One study conducted by David

Newman of the National Cancer Institute in 2003, for example, failed to find a single FDA-approved drug that had originated in combinatorial research. A second study, reported in the *Wall Street Journal* by Peter Landers and quoted by Newman, found that only one of the 350 cancer drugs currently working their way through human trials originated in combinatorial research. The article quoted various researchers and drug company executives who questioned the value of combinatorial techniques as calling the early years of combinatorial chemistry a "nightmare" in which efforts to initiate combinatorial programs have proved to be a "major drag on the development timeline."

Most researchers and drug companies, however, still appear to be confident that combinatorial chemistry holds untold promise for the future. Though they often admit that there is little to show by way of approved products that have evolved from combinatorial techniques, they point out that the early years of new technologies are often marked by similar stories of limited success. Eventually, they say, combinatorial chemistry will take its place with natural products, trial and error, serendipity, and other traditional roads to drug development as an essential tool in the design and production of new pharmaceutical products.

In any case, pharmaceutical companies are not the only places where combinatorial chemistry has been welcomed with enthusiasm and huge investments in new equipment and technology. Combinatorial procedures are also being introduced in the development of new catalysts, novel polymers, advanced materials, and agricultural chemicals. Combinatorial research on new catalysts is a natural extension of work being done on drug development: Just as drugs can be designed to fit into certain types of receptors and enzymes, so catalysts can be designed to provide precise fits for the substrates on which they are supposed to work. For example, researchers at Dow Chemical and Symyx Technologies reported on the development of a library of complexes containing hafnium and zirconium designed to be used in the polymerization of hydrocarbons. They discovered a number of new products with potential application for this industrial field.

Materials science is another field in which combinatorial chemistry has been finding application. The electronics industry, for example, is always on the lookout for new kinds of materials from which smaller and more efficient electronic components can be constructed. In 2000, researchers at Lucent Technologies reported on the search for a new material with a higher dielectric constant (a measure of the ability of a substance to store electric charge) than silicon dioxide, the insulator most commonly used in most kinds of computer chips. In their research, the Lucent scientists synthesized 30 combinatorial libraries, each containing about 4,000 compounds consisting of mixed oxides of zirconium, tin, and titanium. A number of possible candidates in the library were chosen for further analysis and testing.

The future of combinatorial techniques in the fields of drug development and other areas is still not clear. Part of the problem posed by the technology is the dramatic transformation it represents for chemical research. It requires a whole new way of looking at the synthesis of chemical products, and that change will itself bring about the development of entirely new technologies and procedures. Combinatorial chemistry may represent one of the truly great revolutions in the history of chemistry with unimagined success for companies that have chosen to invest in the technology. Or it might prove to result in fewer economically profitable commercial products that its proponents have imagined. As with all new technologies, only the passage of time will tell which of these visions will become reality.

CONCLUSION

The search for chemical compounds that will cure disease, alleviate pain, or otherwise extend human life and make it more comfortable and pleasurable has been a part of human culture as far back as we know. Those who practice forms of traditional medicine have, over the centuries, developed extensive and sophisticated pharmacopoeias that contain many such compounds extracted from plants, animals, and minerals in their surrounding environments. Modern medical researchers have developed their own treasure chests of drugs, many of which have been derived from traditional medicines, and many others of which have been synthesized from basic materials, often by way of complex chemical reactions. Even after thousands of years of drug research, however, healers are not completely satisfied with the armory of chemicals available for their use. People are constantly searching for new compounds that will act more efficiently and more safely than existing pharmaceuticals and for substances with which to combat new forms of disease.

Progress in this campaign of drug research owes much over the past half century to our vastly improved understanding of the chemical basis of living organisms. Scientists now understand the chemical changes that take place in an organism when it becomes ill and, therefore, are able to design more efficiently new chemical compounds with which to combat disease. Amazingly, this development has extended well beyond the range of physical illness and now encompasses a host of mental and emotional disorders.

Problems that once were thought to have been caused by evil spirits, curses, bad luck, or other vague and nonphysical factors have now been shown to result from chemical changes that can be studied, identified, and understood. Every time that kind of progress occurs, a specific method of dealing with a disorder using chemical compounds becomes possible.

None of this, however, is to say that natural products no longer have a role in the modern pharmacopoeia. Indeed, some of the most exciting breakthroughs in medical research in the past half century have resulted from the discoveries of new plant, animal, and mineral products with therapeutic value. Some of these substances have been known and used for centuries by so-called primitive peoples and are just now being discovered by modern medical researchers. Other substances are truly new discoveries, having been identified for the first time by modern investigators tracking down natural products in wild environments.

One of the most exciting areas of drug research is recombinant DNA technology, a field devoted to improved methods of producing traditional drugs (such as insulin) or the development of entirely new drugs related to but different in some important ways from compounds that have long been used in medical science. The use of conventional recombinant techniques, now available for more than a half century, is one way of generating new drugs. The introduction of significantly new methods that make use of domestic animals as "factories" for the production of drugs—the process sometimes called *pharming*—has also shown promise. The procedure has been seen by some observers as a mixed blessing, however, and questions still remain as to how successful pharming techniques will be in the development and production of new and traditional drugs.

Much recent progress in pharmaceutical research has resulted from a rather new approach to the design of drugs, based on the premise that the first step in successful drug design is to attain a sound understanding of the chemical and physical structure of enzymes, cell receptors, disease-causing organisms, and other structures involved in the disease process. Once these structures are known—many researchers now believe—chemists can design and build chemical agonists, compounds that will combine with and inactivate an organism, a molecule, a region of a molecule, or some other structure involved in the disease process.

This philosophy underlies the field of research now known as rational drug design, which includes both structure-activity relationships (SAR) and quantitative structure-activity relationships (QSAR), as well as the exciting new field of combinatorial chemistry. Many individual researchers and pharmaceutical companies are "betting the house" that these new approaches to drug design will lead to the discovery and development of effective new pharmaceuticals in a much shorter time and at significantly less cost than has been the case in the past. Thus far, SAR, QSAR, and combinatorial chemistry have not produced the results generally expected of them. However, they are all relatively new fields of research, and many investigators and investors are willing to wait a while longer to see what great new discoveries will emerge from the use of these techniques.

Any discussion of the chemistry of drugs must include some consideration of the nonmedical applications of such compounds. Just as early humans were searching their environment for natural products that would assuage pain and cure disease, so were they also looking for plants and other natural materials with psychoactive effects, materials that would provide an escape from the problems and worries of everyday life, or that would just make a person feel better for a period of time. They also incorporated psychoactive drugs into many of their religious ceremonies. The use of the peyote cactus, magic mushrooms, and similar products dates back centuries, if not millennia, in a variety of cultures. One hardly need point out that the use of psychoactive chemicals for recreational purposes continues in essentially every part of the world today.

The issue with nonmedical use of drugs today, however, is not only the usual risk involved with the use of any psychoactive drugs but also the increased danger posed by a host of new psychoactive products. Some of these have been developed for legitimate therapeutic purposes, but many of them are spin-offs with unknown effects and, in some cases, known and harmful effects. As pharmaceutical chemists become more imaginative and more successful in designing drugs for the treatment of a whole range of mental and emotional disorders, the availability of such drugs for inappropriate use on the streets becomes much greater. How this nation and the world in general will be able to deal with an ongoing problem of illicit drug use, with the attendant medical problems it brings with it, is a question that has not yet been answered.

◆ GLOSSARY

analog (also **analogue**)   A chemical compound similar in structure to some other chemical compound.

antibiotic   Chemical substances produced by microorganisms or synthesized by chemists that have the capacity in dilute solutions to inhibit the growth of, and/or to destroy, bacteria and other microorganisms.

bioassay   A method of determining the biological effect(s) of a chemical compound by measuring its effect on living organisms or their component parts.

biological activity   The beneficial or adverse effects of a drug on living materials.

biotechnology   Any technological application that uses biological systems, living organisms, or derivatives thereof to make or modify products or processes for specific use (as defined by the Convention on Biological Diversity).

catalyst   A substance that speeds up the rate of a chemical reaction.

chimeric DNA   DNA produced from two genetically different organisms. *See also* RECOMBINANT DNA.

club drug   *See* DESIGNER DRUG.

CNS (central nervous system)   The brain and the spinal cord.

codon   *See* TRIAD.

combinatorial chemistry   A set of procedures by which large numbers of chemical compounds can be synthesized simultaneously.

controlled substance analog (CSA)   *See* DESIGNER DRUG definition (2).

deconvolution   Any one of a number of processes by which the structure of any active compound present in a mixture of compounds is determined.

designer drug   (1) A synthetic chemical compound developed for the treatment of a variety of diseases and disorders. (2) A psychoactive chemical deliberately synthesized to avoid antidrug laws that mimics the effects of a banned drug. Also known as club drug, rave drug, and controlled substance analog.

dimer   A molecule that consists of two identical monomers joined to each other.

disease-directed designer drug   A drug developed to treat some highly specific medical condition.

dissociative anesthesia   A situation in which a person is unaware of pain.

drug   A chemical used in the diagnosis, cure, mitigation, treatment, or prevention of disease or to bring about an alteration in one's mental or emotional state.

efficacy   The effectiveness of a drug to control or cure an illness.

electrophile   A molecule, ion, or other chemical entity that accepts a pair of electrons from some other structure, the NUCLEOPHILE.

enzyme   A protein that increases the rate at which a reaction occurs.

ethnobotany   The study of the way in which cultures use natural products for therapeutic purposes.

fluorous synthesis   A method used in SOLUTION-PHASE SYNTHESIS by which the products of the reactions carried out in that process can be separated from each other.

functional group   An atom or group of atoms responsible for characteristic chemical properties of a family of organic compounds.

genetic engineering   The process by which DNA molecules are modified artificially.

half-life   In pharmacology, the time required for one half of an administered dose to remain in the body.

hallucinogen   A substance that triggers the perception of sights, sounds, or other sensual experiences for the user that do not actually exist or that are not apparent for other people.

indexed library   *See* ORTHOGONAL LIBRARY.

lead compound   A chemical compound that has potential to be developed into a new and useful drug.

library (of compounds)   In combinatorial chemistry, all of the compounds that are produced at approximately the same time in a limited number of chemical reactions.

ligase   An enzyme that catalyzes the formation of covalent bonds.

linker   A functional group used in solid-phase synthesis to join the solid support (such as a resin bead) to the first monomer used in forming a polymer.

molecular farming   *See* PHARMING.

monomer   A single small molecule able to combine with other molecules of the same kind to make large compounds known as polymers.

multipin system   A method of solid-phase synthesis in which synthesis takes place on tiny pins made of some appropriate polymeric material.

multiple parallel synthesis   *See* SOLUTION-PHASE SYNTHESIS.

neuron   A nerve cell.

neurotransmitter   A chemical that carries a nerve impulse between two neurons.

nucleophile   A molecule, ion, or other chemical structure that donates a pair of electrons to some other substance, the **electrophile.**

nucleoside   The combination of a sugar and a nitrogen base.

nucleotide   The combination of a sugar, nitrogen base, and phosphate group.

oligonucleotide   A polymer consisting of a few nucleotide units, "few" generally meaning less than about two dozen.

opiate receptors   Specialized receptor cells in neurons that bind to natural analgesic (painkilling) molecules present in the body.

orphan drug   A drug used to treat a rare disease, "rare" meaning one that affects relatively few people (in the United States, less than 200,000), for which a pharmaceutical firm cannot expect to cover the costs of its research and development on the drug in a reasonable period of time.

orthogonal library   In combinatorial chemistry, a mechanism for carrying out the synthesis of many compounds at the same time by which the characteristic properties of one or more of those compounds can be identified. Also known as an indexed library.

parallel synthesis   *See* SOLUTION-PHASE SYNTHESIS.

Parkinson's disease   A degenerative disease of the nervous system characterized by tremor and impaired muscular coordination.

patient-directed designer drug   A drug developed to meet the medical needs of very specific types of individuals.

pharmacopoeia   A catalog of drugs, chemicals, and medicinal preparations.

pharmacogenomics   The study of the way in which individuals respond to various drugs because of their unique genetic makeup.

pharmacophore   The physical and chemical structure of some fundamental part of a molecule that binds to an enzyme, a cell receptor, or some other biological target to produce a biological effect.

pharming   A modern field of technology in which traditional methods of farming are used for the production of pharmaceutical chemicals. Also known as MOLECULAR FARMING.

phenylethylamine   A member of a family of organic compounds that contains three primary functional groups: the phenyl ($-C_6H_5$) group, ethyl ($-C_2H_5$) group, and amino ($-NH_2$) group.

plasmid   A small, circular piece of DNA, found in bacteria and capable of autonomous reproduction.

polyprotein   *See* SUPERPROTEIN.

rave drug   *See* DESIGNER DRUG.

receptor molecule   A molecule to which some other molecule, ion, or chemical entity binds.

recombinant DNA   DNA that has been produced by joining genetic material from two different sources. Also, the process by which this type of DNA is produced. Also known as chimeric DNA.

resin bead   A small spherical object, usually made of a polymer such as cross-linked polyethylene, used as the solid support in a solid-phase synthesis experiment.

restriction endonuclease   *See* RESTRICTION ENZYME.

restriction enzyme   An enzyme that recognizes certain sequences of nitrogen bases and breaks the bonds at some point within that sequence. Also known as a *restriction endonuclease.*

scavenger resin   A polymer that has been especially designed to react with excess reactant, by-products, or other species present in a reaction that must be removed in order to obtain a pure product.

schedule (drug)   A category into which the federal government classifies certain drugs, based on their potential medical use and their possibility for illicit use.

solid-phase synthesis   One of the most common methods of combinatorial chemistry, by which large numbers of compounds are produced simultaneously while anchored to some kind of solid support, such as a resin bead.

solution-phase synthesis   A common form of combinatorial chemistry in which large numbers of compounds are produced simultaneously in reactions carried out in a solution-phase. Also called parallel synthesis or multiple parallel synthesis.

species   In chemistry, a general term used to describe any type of particle, such as atoms, molecules, ions, or fragments of these particles.

split and mix system (of solid-phase synthesis)   A method of making large numbers of compounds simultaneously on solid supports in which the components are first separated from each other, then split into separate parts, then recombined, and so on.

structure-activity relationships   A field of drug synthesis in which the physical shape of a receptor site, enzyme substrate, or other biological structure is used for the design of a new drug.

substance P   A substance thought to be responsible for the transmission of pain messages in the body.

substituent   An atom or group of atoms inserted into a molecule in place of some other atom (often hydrogen) or group of atoms.

substrate   The portion of a molecule, cell, organism, or some other structure on which an enzyme operates.

superprotein   A long-chain molecule that contains within itself subunits, each of which has some important biological function. Also known as a polyprotein.

synaptic gap   The space between two neurons.

temporary unrousable unconsciousness   A type of coma that can be life-threatening.

transgenic organism   An organism that contains DNA from some second organism that has been transplanted into it.

triad   A set of three nitrogen bases in an RNA or DNA molecule that codes for a specific amino acid. Also called a codon.

vector (biological)   An agent, such as a plasmid or a virus, used to transplant a gene into a host organism.

◆ FURTHER READING

PRINT

Abraham, Donald J. *Burger's Medicinal Chemistry and Drug Discovery.* 6th ed. 6 vol. New York: Wiley-Interscience, 2003.

Aldridge, Susan. *Magic Molecules: How Drugs Work.* Cambridge: Cambridge University Press, 1998.

Bannworth, Willi, and Eduard Felder, eds. *Combinatorial Chemistry: A Practical Approach.* Weinheim, Germany: Wiley-VCH, 2000.

Buchanan, J. F. "'Designer Drugs.' A Problem in Clinical Toxicology," *Medical Toxicology and Adverse Drug Experience* (January/December 1988): 1–17.

Cabri, Walter, and Romano De Fabio. *From Bench to Market: The Evolution of Chemical Synthesis.* New York: Oxford University Press, 2000.

Dye, Christina. *Drugs and the Body: How Drugs Work.* Tempe, Ariz.: Do It Now Foundation, 1997. Also available online at http://www.doitnow.org/pdfs/223.pdf.

Fletcher, Andrew J., et al., eds. *Principles and Practice of Pharmaceutical Medicine.* New York: John Wiley & Sons, 2002.

Heinrich, M., and S. Gibbons. "Ethnopharmacology in Drug Discovery: An Analysis of Its Role and Potential Contribution," *Journal of Pharmacy and Pharmacology* vol. 53, no. 4, April 2001: 425–432.

Henderson, Gary. "Designer Drugs: The New Synthetic Drugs of Abuse," in A. Church and F. Sapienza, *Proceedings of Controlled Substance Analog Leadership Conference.* Washington, D.C.: U.S. Department of Justice, Drug Enforcement Administration, Office of Diversion Control, 1986.

Hilisch, A., and R. Hilgenfeld, eds. *Modern Methods of Drug Discovery.* Basel: Birkhäuser Verlag, 2003.

Jenkins, Philip. *Synthetic Panics: The Symbolic Politics of Designer Drugs.* New York: New York University Press, 1999.

Jollès, P., ed. *New Approaches to Drug Development.* Basel: Birkhäuser Verlag, 2000.

Jungmittag, Andre, Guido Reger, and Thomas Reiss, eds. *Changing Innovation in the Pharmaceutical Industry: Globalization and New Ways of Drug Development.* Berlin: Springer, 2000.

Landers, Peter. "Drug Industry's Big Push into Technology Falls Short," *Wall Street Journal,* February 24, 2004. Also available online at http://www.mindfully.org/GE/2004/Drug-Industry-Falls-Short24feb04.htm.

Makiryannis, Alexandros, and Diane Biegel. *Drug Discovery Strategies and Methods.* New York: Marcel Dekker, 2004.

Maulik, Sunil, and Salil D. Patel. *Molecular Biotechnology: Therapeutic Applications and Strategies.* New York: Wiley-Liss, 1997.

McGavock, Hugh. *How Drugs Work: Basic Pharmacology for Healthcare Professionals.* Abingdon, U.K.: Radcliffe Medical Press, 2002.

Ng, Rick. *Drugs: From Discovery to Approval.* Hoboken, N.J.: Wiley-Liss, 2004.

Oxender, Dale L., and Leonard E. Post. *Novel Therapeutics from Modern Biotechnology: From Laboratory to Human Testing.* Berlin: Springer, 1999.

Rintoul, Scott, and Christy MacKilliean. *Designer Drugs and Raves.* 2nd ed. Vancouver, B.C.: National Crime Prevention Council, 2001. Also available online at http://www.rcmp-fairmont.org/da/docs/rave.pdf.

Rouhi, A. Maureen. "Rediscovering Natural Products." *Chemical & Engineering News* vol. 81, no. 41, October 13, 2003, pp. 77–78+. Also available online at http://pubs.acs.org/cen/coverstory/8141/8141pharmaceuticals.html.

Scientific Section (Laboratory), Policy Development and Analysis Branch, Division for Operations and Analysis. *Terminology and Information on Drugs.* 2nd ed. Vienna: United Nations, Office on Drugs and Crime, 1998.

Seneci, Pierfausto. *Solid Phase Synthesis and Combinatorial Technologies.* New York: John Wiley & Sons, 2000.

Shulgin, Alexander T., and D. E. Nichols. "Characterization of three new psychotomimetics," in R. C. Stillman and R. E. Willette, *The Pharmacology of Hallucinogens,* New York: Pergamon, 1978.

———, and Ann Shulgin. *PiHKAL: A Chemical Love Story.* Berkeley, Calif.: Transform Press, 1991.

———. *TiHKAL: The Continuation.* Berkeley, Calif.: Transform Press, 1997.

Terrett, Nicholas K. *Combinatorial Chemistry.* Oxford: Oxford University Press, 1998.

Thiericke, R., and S. Grabley, eds. *Drug Discovery from Nature.* Berlin: Springer, 1999.

Thomas, Gareth. *Medicinal Chemistry: An Introduction.* Chichester, U.K.: John Wiley & Sons, 2000.

Torrence, Paul F., ed. *Biomedical Chemistry: Applying Chemical Principles to the Understanding and Treatment of Disease.* New York: John Wiley & Sons, 2000.

Torssell, Kurt B. *Natural Product Chemistry: A Mechanistic and Biosynthetic Approach to Secondary Metabolism.* Chichester, U.K.: John Wiley & Sons, 1983.

Tringali, Corrado, ed. *Bioactive Compounds from Natural Sources: Isolation, Characterisation and Biological Properties.* London: Taylor & Francis, 2001.

INTERNET

a1b2c3.com. "Recreational Drugs Information." a1b2c3.com. Available online. URL: http://www.a1b2c3.com/drugs/. Downloaded on August 17, 2005.

ARBEC. "Biotechnology and Natural Products," ASEAN Review of Biodiversity and Environmental Conservation. Available online. URL: http://www.arbec.com.my/biotech.htm. Posted on March 14, 2001.

Batchelder, Tim. "Natural Products from the Sea: Ethnopharmacology, Nutrition and Conservation," FindArticles.com. Available online. URL: http://articles.findarticles.com/p/articles/mi_m0ISW/is_2001_Feb/ai_70777319. Originally in *Townsend Letter for Doctors and Patients* 211 (February 2001): 136–141.

BBC Science & Nature. "Plant Pharming," BBC. Available online. URL: http://www.bbc.co.uk/science/genes/gene_safari/pharm/plant_p.shtml. Downloaded on August 16, 2005.

Betsch, David F. "Pharmaceutical Production from Transgenic Animals," Biotechnology Information Series, Iowa State University Extension and Office of Biotechnology. Available online. URL: http://www.biotech.iastate.edu/biotech_info_series/bio10.html. Updated on June 28, 2001.

Bevan, David R. "QSAR and Drug Design," Network Science, Department of Biochemistry and Aerobic Microbiology, Virginia Polytechnic Institute and State University. Available online. URL: http://www.netsci.org/Science/Compchem/feature12.html. Posted January 1996.

Center for Emerging Issues. "Animal Pharming: The Industrialization of Transgenic Animals," Animal and Plant Health Inspection Service. Available online. URL: http://www.aphis.usda.gov/vs/ceah/cei/animal_pharming.htm. Posted December 1999.

Center for Science in the Public Interest. "The Future of Pharming: Can It Be Done Safely?" Transcript of a CSPI conference on emerging technologies, held December 17, 2002. Available online. URL: http://www.cspinet.org/new/200212301.html. Posted on December 30, 2002.

Cooper, Donald A. "Future Synthetic Drugs of Abuse," Designer-Drugs.com. Available online. URL: http://designer-drugs.com/synth/index.html. Downloaded on August 16, 2005.

Cunningham, A. B. "Ethics, Biodiversity, and New Natural Product Development," People and Plants Online. Available online. URL: http://peopleandplants.org/web-content/web-content%201/dp/dp2/index.html. Downloaded on September 5, 2006.

DEA. "DEA Resources for Law Enforcement Officers," U.S. Drug Enforcement Administration. Available online. URL: http://www.usdoj.gov/dea/pubs/. Downloaded on August 16, 2005.

Erowid. "Psychoactive Chemicals," Erowid. Available online. URL: http://www.erowid.org/chemicals. Updated on August 16, 2005.

Gerritz, Samuel W. "Whither Solid Phase Synthesis?" Current Drug Discovery. Available online. URL: http://www.currentdrugdiscovery.com/pdf/2002/6/gerritz.pdf. Posted June 2002.

Gillespie, David. "Pharming for Farmaceuticals," Genetic Science Learning Center at the University of Utah. Available online. http://gslc.genetics. utah.edu/features/pharming/. Downloaded on August 16, 2005.

The Menarini Group. "Birth of a Drug," The Menarini Group. Available online. URL: http://www.menarini.com/english/ricerca_sviluppo/ farmaco.htm. Downloaded on August 16, 2005.

Mitscher, Lester A., and Apurba Dutta. "Combinatorial Chemistry and Multiple Parallel Synthesis," John Wiley & Sons, Inc. Available online. URL: http://media.wiley.com/product_data/excerpt/82/04713702/ 0471370282.pdf. Originally published in *Burger's Medicinal Chemistry and Drug Discovery,* edited by Donald J. Abraham. Vol. 2, *Drug Discovery and Development.* Hoboken, N.J.: Wiley, 2003.

National Institute on Drug Abuse. "Ecstasy: What We Know and Don't Know About MDMA: A Scientific Review," National Institute on Drug Abuse. Available online. URL: http://www.nida.nih.gov/PDF/ MDMAConf.pdf. Updated on February 2, 2005.

PBS Online. "Animations: How Drugs Work," PBS Online: Close to Home. Available online. URL: http://www.pbs.org/wnet/closetohome/ science/html/animations.html. Downloaded on September 5, 2006.

Pew Initiative on Food and Biotechnology, et al. "Pharming the Field," proceedings of a workshop held July 17–18, 2002. Available online. URL: http://pewagbiotech.org/events/0717/ConferenceReport.pdf. Posted on February 28, 2003.

Shulgin, Alexander, "Utopian Pharmacology," Erowid. Available online. URL: http://www.mdma.net/index.html. Downloaded on September 5, 2006.

Sneden, Albert T. "Natural Products as Medicinally Useful Agents," Leaf Squeezers Web. Available online. URL: http://www.people.vcu.edu/ ~asneden/MEDC%20310%20Intro.htm. Updated June 21, 2005.

Walters, D. Eric. "Where Do New Drugs Come From?" Department of Biochemistry & Molecular Biology, Rosalind Franklin University. Available online. URL: http://www.finchcms.edu/cms/biochem/ walters/walters_lect/walters_lect.html. Downloaded on August 17, 2005.

INDEX